# A STRAIGHTFORWARD GUIDE TO INDIVIDUAL AND FAMILY FINANCES

ADRIAN FELLOWS

Straightforward Publishing
www.straightforwardco.co.uk

Straightforward Publishing limited
Brighton BN1 6AA



British Library Cataloguing in Publication Data. A Catalogue record for this book is available from the British Library.

ISBN 1 903909 58 9

Printed and bound by Antony Rowe Ltd, Eastbourne

Cover design by Straightforward Graphics

CONTENTS

*Chapter 1*
*Financial Advice* *13*

Different types of advisors 13
Tied advisers 13
Multi-Tied advisers 14
Independent advisers 14
Qualifications and regulations 14
Commission and fees 15
Services offered by different advisers 16
Complaints 19
Complaint schemes generally 20
The Financial Ombudsman Service 19
The Office for the Pensions Advisory Service 20
The Pensions Ombudsman 20
The Mortgage Code Arbitration Scheme 20
The General Insurance Standards Council 20
The Ombudsman for Estate Agents 21
The Financial Services Compensation Scheme 21
Pensions Compensation Board 21

*Chapter 2*
*Mortgages* *23*

The options available 23
Various methods of repayment 26
Associated costs of buying property 33

*Chapter 3*
*Buying and selling your home* *37*

Buying 37
Selling 38

*Chapter 4*
*Life insurance* *39*

Do you need it? 39
Different types of life insurance 40
Decreasing term insurance 40
Level term insurance 41
Family Income Benefit policy 41
Whole Life insurance 42
Critical Illness 42

*Chapter 5*
*Saving* *45*

Cash returns 46
Tax on interest earned 47
The choice of accounts 47
Children's accounts 48
Instant access accounts 48
Internet accounts 48
Mini-isas 48
Monthly income accounts 49
Notice accounts 49
Postal accounts 49
Telephone accounts 49
Time deposits 49

Fixed-rate investments 50
Short-term fixed-rate investments 50
Escalator bonds 50
Fixed rate bonds 50
Guaranteed growth bonds 50
Guaranteed income bonds 51
Maxi-isas 51
National savings certificates 51
National savings pensioners guaranteed bonds 51
Longer term savings plans 51
With profits savings plans 52
Friendly society plans 53
The purpose of saving 54

*Chapter 6*
*Single premium and lump sum investments* *55*

The options available 56
Tax implications 59

*Chapter 7*
*Income protection* *61*

Cover offered by banks and building societies 62

*Chapter 8*
*Pensions* *63*

The State Pension Scheme (SERPS) 64
Personal pension plans for self employed 64
Personal pension plans for the employed 66

Occupational pension schemes 67
Pension transfers 68

*Chapter 9*
*Stocks and shares* *69*

Today's stock market 69
Shareholders and shares 70
Recognising a good business 71
Choosing an investment style 72
Value investing 72
Growth investing 73
The life cycle views 73
Stockbrokers services 74
Cutting losses as an individual investor 75
Researching companies 76
Investment clubs 76

*Chapter 10* *77*
*Tax*

Tax generally 77
Income Tax 79
The employed 88
The self-employed 79
Capital Gains Tax 80
Inheritance tax 80
Exemptions 81
Gifts made before death 81

*Chapter 11*
*Wills and Trusts* *83*

If a will is not made 83
Changing your will 84
Benefits of making a will 84
Trusts 87

*Chapter 12*
*Borrowing money* *87*

Caution before borrowing 87
Comparison of costs 88
Payment protection insurance 89
Borrowing to pay off other loans 89
Overdrafts 89
Credit cards 89
Personal loans 90
Secured or unsecured loans 91
Interest free or low-start credit 91
Hire purchase 92
Credit unions 92
Credit scoring 93

*Chapter 13*
*Education* *95*

Bursaries, Scholarships and help 97
University education 97
Current costs of university 98
Future costs 98
Student loan company 98

*Chapter 14*
*Health Care* *101*

Private medical care 101
Regulatory structure 103
Long term care 104
LTC insurance 104
Immediate needs policy 105
Regulation 106

*Chapter 15*
*Funeral costs* *107*

*Chapter 16*
*The Costs of Getting Married* *109*

*Useful addresses* *113*

# INTRODUCTION

The main purpose of this book is to guide the reader through the maze of personal financial decisions which he or she or the family might have to make during a lifetime.

I have concentrated heavily on specific areas such as pensions, savings and insurance, because these are areas which will have the most effect on you during the course of your working life. There are also frequent references to financial advisors, ranging from the independent advisor to those employed by institutions such as banks. I have made repeated references because very often you will receive advice from such a person and will make decisions based on that advice.

As an individual, you could spend untold hours the various options open to you with regard to financial matters, only to find yourself more confused than ever due to conflicting advice received along the way. That advice will, quite often, be made in the best interests of the advisor, and his or her subsequent commissions, rather than in the best interests of yourself.

A Straightforward Guide to Individual and Family Finances will set out, in a clear and unambiguous way, the meaning and implications of the various financial options open to you, and should leave you in a better position to make an informed choice.

The main areas covered by the book are mortgages, life insurance, savings, investments, income protection, pensions, tax wills and trusts, other personal options for investment such as stocks and shares. In addition, I have covered education, health care, weddings and funerals.

Because of the importance of receiving accurate advice from financial advisors, the book will begin by outlining the law that governs such advisors and also the types of advice given.

# 1
# Financial Advice

There are many ways to purchase financial products nowadays, either through the Internet or by telephone. However, when considering more complex financial issues, it is evident that professional advice is needed. There are numerous advantages to using financial advisors, one of the main ones being that you will have extra protection if things go wrong. The first step towards finding a good advisor is considering which type is likely to provide the service you need. Like solicitors and other professionals, financial advisors do specialise and you would have to find the correct advisor for your needs. It is also very important to discover whether or not the advisor is properly authorised and registered and approved by the correct bodies. Nowadays, advisors and the companies that they work for must be authorised by the financial services watchdog, the Financial Services Authority (FSA). To be on the safe side you should always check with the FSA. You can also find out what type of business the advisor is authorised to do. These details are held on the FSA's register. Its public enquiries helpline is on 0845 606 1234. It is important to be aware of the distinctions between different types of advisors, the services they are likely to provide, and how they are likely to be paid, before narrowing your choice down.

## Different types of advisers

Until recently, financial advisors were divided into two clear groups – tied and independent. The distinction was blurred by the introduction of multi-tied advisors to sell stakeholder pensions. Now the FSA is planning further changes in the way advisors are categorised. However, at present, the main categories of advisor are:

## Tied

These individuals work for a particular company and can only sell you the products offered by that company. Employees of banks and insurance companies fall into this category. However, many small firms of self-employed financial consultants have the same status.

There is nothing wrong with buying financial products this way. Some of the lowest cost products are sold by tied agents. They also, however, sell some of the poorest value products. You should make your own comparisons of the value of their products and also of the charges and overall performance.

## Multi-tied

This type of advisor acts as distributor for a limited range of companies. This will enable them to offer a choice of, for example, several different pension plans. However, again, they may not be the best available. You should ensure that you are seeing as wide a range as possible of products before making your choice.

## Independent

These advisers can advise you on any company's products. They are required to make their recommendations based on the basic principles of 'best advice' and 'best execution'. This means that they should advise you which products are the best to meet your particular needs, and if there are a number of providers of these they should shop around to find best value. They do not have to recommend the cheapest product on the market if there are good reasons to recommend something else more suitable.

## Qualifications and regulations

All financial advisers must have a level of qualification. To be registered, they must have passed the three levels of the Financial

Planning Certificate (FPC) exam, or equivalent. The next stage for them is to take various levels of the Advanced Financial Planning Certificate (AFPC). Advisers who have passed ten subjects at AFPC level are regarded as among the best qualified.

Specialist advisers may have other relevant qualifications or be members of various professional bodies. Companies and advisers who are registered with the FSA must report regularly to the regulator and their affairs and business generally is inspected on a periodic basis by the regulators representatives. If a company or advisor does not meet the standards used to measure performance a fine can be imposed or an adviser's authorisation removed. The inspector can also tell the company to retrain their workforce.

**Commission or fees**

Advice from Financial Advisors does not generally come free. There are several ways in which a financial advisor can be paid.

**Commission**

Traditionally, most advisers have received commission for selling packaged financial products, such as insurance policies, pensions and savings plans. Although the financial institution offering the product pays the commission, this comes out of your money. The main advantage of this approach is that customers who do not have any capital can still obtain advice.

The commission-based approach has also had some very detrimental side effects. It has led unscrupulous advisors to recommend products because they paid high levels of commission rather than because they were the best choice for investor. This has been the main complaint against financial advisors in the past and has led to the industry being tightened up.

Another disadvantage with regular savings products, such as endowments or friendly society plans, is that the main part of the commission is often paid to the adviser as soon as the product is sold. As the amount of commission is often based on the term of the product, this meant large deductions being made initially sometimes absorbing the first few years' contributions. Although, by the end of the term the effect can be smoothed out, problems will arise if the saver stops paying into the contract for some reason.

Increasing regulation of financial advisors is helping to put an end to these practices. Nowadays, advisors have to provide key features documents when they sell investment products. Increasing regulation has meant greater transparency and more communication from advisor to client.

### Fees

Some professional advisors, such as stockbrokers, accountants and solicitors have always charged fees. Under recent FSA proposals, financial advisors who want to call themselves 'independent' may be forced to do the same. The advantage of fees as opposed to commission is that the advisor is under no pressure to sell you any product at all and may be prepared to advise you about products that do not pay any commission.

For larger investors, paying fees can actually save money. Even though fee based advisors may charge upwards of £125 per hour, the final bill may still be less that commission based on a percentage of the amount invested.

## Services offered by different advisers

### Accountants

Accountants are usually the best source of advice on tax matters. Some can also advise on investments provided that they are authorised by the FSA. Some of the larger accountancy forms have specialist independent financial advice departments to provide a full planning service. You will have to pay a fee to accountants for such advice but any commission generated by sales of products is usually offset against the final bill.

For names of local accountants contact the Institute of Chartered Accountants, the Association of Chartered certified Accountants or the Chartered Institute of Taxation and Association of Tax Technicians (see appendix).

**Actuaries**

Actuaries are normally employed by insurance companies but there are also firms of independent consultants who can be approached for specialist advice on insurance related matter such as pension transfers. They work on a fee basis. The Association of Consulting Actuaries can provide you with the name of a firm in your area.

**Banks and building societies**

Most larger banks and building societies have in-house financial consultants who are tied agents. In the future, some banks may become multi-tied and start offering the products of several companies but their range will still remain limited. Some banks offer advice through private arms designed for wealthier customers (with more than £100,000 to invest for example).

**Company representatives**

Many insurance companies have their own sales forces to promote their products and services. Traditional insurers, such as Legal and General and the Co-operative still employ hundreds of representatives who will visit people in their own homes to discuss their needs.

Companies selling direct by telephone also use their own representatives.

**Independent financial advisors**

All IFA's can sell the products of any company in the market that they choose. However, there are considerable variations in the services they can offer. Some are small, often one-man operations, some belong to national networks, and some are nationwide companies. Many are 'general practitioners' dealing mainly with packaged products, such as life insurance, pension products and unit trusts. Others offer more extensive financial planning whilst others specialise in particular areas, such as mortgages or investments. Although most IFA's are paid commission, many offer a choice nowadays and will work on a fee basis if clients prefer.

If you are looking for local, reputable financial advisers you can contact IFA promotion. For fee based independent advisers, contact the Money management Directory of fee based advisers. Organisations that promote professional development amongst their members are the Society of Financial Advisors (SOFA) and the Institute of Financial Planning. SOFA is the financial services arm of the Chartered Insurance Institute. It has three categories of membership depending on how many levels of the Advanced Planning Certificate (AFPC) advisors have achieved.

**Solicitors**

If you need legal advice on certain matters such as dealing with wills and probate, you will need to consult a firm of solicitors. They may also be able to provide financial planning and investment advice on a fee basis. There are two organisations that represent solicitors offering these services. They are the Association of Solicitor Investment Managers (ASIM) and Solicitors for Independent Investment Advice. If you have a legal problem relating to a pension, you should contact the Association of Pension Lawyers. See appendix for details.

## Stockbrokers

Stockbrokers have become more accessible over the years, particularly recently. Many of the newer telephone based services cater mainly for investors who know which shares they want to buy and sell, and they do not provide advice other than general information bulletins. However, many firms still offer advisory and discretionary management services. For smaller investors, a unit or investment manage trust management may be offered.

To find out which stockbrokers offer these services to private clients, contact the Association of Private Client Investment Managers and Stockbrokers (APCIMS). It has a free directory of member firms, many of which provide a full financial planning service. See appendix for details.

## Tied agents

Tied agents are also known as 'appointed representatives'. These are self-employed consultants or companies, which have a contract to sell one or more of an insurance company's products or commission. The agent may operate independently in respect of other business. For example, many building societies are tied agents and will sell the investment and investment products of one insurance company.

## Complaints

If you are unhappy with a financial product or service, you have the means to complain. As with many complaints, you must first give the company the chance to put things right. If this cannot be achieved then there are other routes, such as the Financial Ombudsman Service.

However, before the Ombudsman will take up your complaint you must be able to show that you have followed the company complaint procedure and have still received no satisfactory solution to your problem.

## Complaints schemes generally

**The Financial Ombudsman Service.** This provides a single complaints scheme divided into three specialist divisions for banking and loans, insurance and investments. It covers the following types of companies and organisations:

- Banks
- Building societies
- Financial advisors
- Firms dealing in futures and options/ Friendly Societies
- Fund managers
- Life insurance companies
- Pension providers
- Stockbrokers

**The Office for the Pensions Advisory Service**. OPAS provides initial advice and conciliation for complaints about employers pension schemes.

**The Pensions Ombudsman**. This ombudsman decides on complaints relating to employers pension schemes not resolved by OPAS.

**The Mortgage Code Arbitration Scheme**. This deals with complaints about mortgage intermediaries such as brokers and estate agents.

**The general Insurance Standards Council**. This is a voluntary scheme handling complaints about general insurance brokers such as those selling motor and household cover.

**The Ombudsman for Estate agents**. This is a voluntary scheme dealing with complaints about estate agents from both buyers and sellers. About a third of agencies are members.

## Protection

If you lose money due to miss-selling or misadministration, an ombudsman may be able to ensure that you get financial compensation. However, if fraud is apparent, this may not be possible, or if the company or individual becomes bankrupt.

## The Financial Services Compensation Scheme

The maximum amounts of compensation are as follows:

- Deposits 100% of the first £2000 and 90% of the next £33,000 per individual (maximum £31,700)
- General Insurance Compulsory claims – 100%. Non-compulsory claims-100% of first £2000 and 90% of the rest.
- Long-term insurance 90% of the value of the policy, including future benefits.
- Investments 100% of the first £30,000 and 90% of the next £20,000. (maximum £48.000).

## Pensions Compensation Board

This covers member liabilities of occupational pensions in full.

Offshore compensation

Investors should bear in mind that these schemes do not apply to firms based outside the United Kingdom. Although some offshore investment centres, such as the Isle of Man, may have their own compensation schemes, others do not. When investing outside the UK take great care to gain as much information as possible from the institution concerned.

# 2
# Mortgages

## The options available

There comes a time in almost everyone's life when they need to leave the family home and establish their own independence. The majority cannot afford to buy a property immediately and so enter some form of rented accommodation, depending on circumstances. For those who wish to buy a property then the normal route is through obtaining a mortgage, unless you are fortunate to possess enough cash to purchase outright.

In recent years, the attitude of banks and building societies and other financial institutions has radically changed as they are all keen to lend you as much money as possible, subject to status (how much you earn)

In order to establish how much money you could borrow, the general criteria is as follows:

a) 2.5 x joint income;
b) 3 x higher income plus the lower income;
c) up to 3.5 x single income.

However, because of spiraling house prices, most lenders will lens more and some will lend over longer terms such as 35 years

.

Most building societies will lend a maximum of 95% of the purchase price of the property. It is important to remember that in order to gain a mortgage you must be credit worthy, have a steady or regular income and be confident in your ability to maintain such an important financial commitment.

Once you are aware of how much you can borrow, the difficult decision of deciding what type of mortgage you want has to be made. The options are many. However, there are a number of main ones which are outlined below:

The Variable Rate Mortgage
The Discounted Rate Mortgage
The Fixed Rate Mortgage
The Capped Rate Mortgage
The Deferred Rate Mortgage
Cashbacks

The variable rate mortgage is the most common, with the majority of borrowers preferring this type of loan. You will pay the rate of interest charged by the lender as standard and any increases or decreases in that rate will be reflected in your monthly payments.

**Discounted Rate Mortgage**
A discounted rate is usually offered by lenders to attract new business. They may offer a straight discount off the variable rate currently in force for a period of 1, 2 or 3 years after which time the rate of interest will simply revert to the standard interest rate at that particular time.

It is important to note that a discount of 1% for three years is 1% off the variable rate and therefore this will fluctuate as the variable rate changes.

**Fixed Rate Mortgage**
A fixed rate will guarantee that your mortgage payments will remain the same throughout the fixed rate period. After this time, your mortgage will simply revert to the standard variable rate. It is normal with any fixed rate that you will be charged a fee by the lender for the benefit of a fixed rate. It is always worth

considering a fixed rate especially if the variable rate is low, as you will get a good rate of interest for a period of 2-10 years. With any fixed rate if you decide to sell your property within the fixed period you can be charged a redemption penalty, but most are portable and you can take the interest rate with you if you move property.

## Capped rate mortgages

A capped rate mortgage means that your mortgage repayments may reduce below a certain level but will never go above that level during the capped rate period. This is very similar to a fixed rate but with the added advantage of the possibility of the payments going down. Once again, a fee is normally charged and redemption penalties are the same as the fixed rate.

## Deferred Mortgages

A deferred mortgage is a very complicated means by which to repay a loan. Quite simply, it was very popular when rates were 15% and people were struggling to maintain their payments. It is easier to explain with the illustration below:

Mortgage £100,000<br>
Interest rate 8%<br>
Deferred 25%<br>
Mortgage repayments on interest only £666.66 (gross)<br>
£40 tax relief<br>
£626.66 total<br>
-25% deferred<br>
£156.67 x 12 = £1880.04 increase after one year<br>
£469.99 net.

The difference gets compounded and added onto the loan, therefore after the deferral period, the mortgage balance has increased drastically and the mortgage payments could increase out of control. This type of mortgage is not recommended to anyone unless they expect a substantial change in income over a 3-5 year term.

### Cash backs

In addition to all of the above mortgage options, most of the major lenders try to entice you to borrow from them by offering a cash incentive. For example, if you want a discounted rate, they may offer you a refund of your survey fee and possibly some additional money towards your legal expenses. If, however, you decided that you wanted to borrow at the normal rate of interest, some lenders may offer you a cash incentive of up to 7% of your advance. Like most other mortgages, you can find yourself penalised if you decide to transfer your mortgage in the earlier years.

### Various methods of repayment

As if you did not have enough to think about, once you have decided on what mortgage you are going to have, it is now time to decide on how you are going to pay it back.

Traditionally, banks and building societies only lend money on the repayment method. However, with a change in the general wealth of the country and the significant increase in the number of people able to buy property, the industry quickly adopted new methods in order to meet the requirements of the individuals.

There are now five main types of repayments attached to mortgages:

Repayment
Endowment
Pension
ISA (Individual savings account)
Interest only

## Repayment

When you borrow money on a repayment basis your repayments are made up of interest and capital, so that after each year you should see a slight reduction in the capital. After the 25-year period the mortgage is repaid and the property is owned outright.

## Advantages of a repayment mortgage

If you intend to stay in the property for the full term you will be guaranteed to repay your loan. If you are approaching your late 40s and onwards, a repayment would probably be the cheapest option. You can also pay extra towards the mortgage to reduce the capital.

## Disadvantages of a repayment mortgage

The interest is added onto the loan at the beginning so if you decide to move within the first ten years there will be no significant reduction in the capital. When you decide to move, the mortgage is not "portable" so you will have to start a further 25 years to reduce the term, but you will find the repayments a lot more expensive.

## The Endowment mortgage

An endowment mortgage consists of two parts: the interest payable on the loan and premiums on the endowment. The purpose of the endowment is to grow, through regular contributions, to an extent where at the end of the mortgage term the value of the policy is sufficient to pay off the mortgage. If the insurance company has invested well you may receive a tax-free lump sum as well.

There are two main types of endowment: unit linked and low cost endowments. The main difference between the two can be attributed to risk and your attitude to that risk.

### Low cost endowment

This is the traditional endowment which has been used to repay mortgages since endowments were introduced. The risk is moderate because your premiums are invested in low risk investments and each year you receive a bonus which is added to your policy and cannot be taken away.

The bonuses are directly determined by the profit made by the company. At the end of the mortgage term the insurance company will give you a final bonus which will normally bring the value of the policy equal to, if not greater than, the mortgage.

As part of your endowment, you have life cover so that in the event of a fatality during the term of the policy, provided premiums have been maintained, a lump sum equivalent to the sum assured will be paid. Waiver of premium can be taken out as part of your endowment contract which would give you added protection in the event of not being able to work due to accident or sickness. The waiver benefit would pay your endowment premiums after 6 months of the claim and until such time as you would be able to return to your regular job.

Most endowment premiums remain constant throughout the term of the mortgage. There is however a low start endowment which would allow the cost of the endowment to drop significantly for the initial 3 or 4 years of the policy.

A new concept in the endowment range is the benefit of critical illness or serious illness protection. See life insurance further on in this book.

### The unit-linked endowment

The purpose of the unit-linked endowment is exactly the same as the low cost endowment and that is to repay the mortgage at the end of the term. There are, however, fundamental differences in the way the money is invested, the bonus structure and the risk involved with this type of investment. The unit-linked endowment also has various additional contract options which are unique to the unit linked market.

### How the money is invested

The Fund Managers will research the markets to establish where they can invest your money over the medium to long term in order to gain an investment return of above average performance. The investments can range from UK Securities to Overseas Quoted Equities, Fixed Interest, Property and Cash. As the scope for investment is so great it is important that you are always aware of the risk factors involved as they can vary quite drastically.

### Bonus structure

The value of the policy is purely dependent on the value of the units in the various funds. Unit prices go up and down and therefore the value of the policy changes on a daily basis.

### Additional benefits

Segmentation: A unit-linked endowment is written in clusters, normally ten and at any stage an individual part of the policy can be surrendered.

Early redemption: most endowments are expected to exceed the mortgage after 25 years, there is therefore the opportunity to redeem the mortgage earlier, should the value of the policy equal the mortgages.

### Summary: the endowment method

### Advantages

- Guaranteed life cover during mortgage term.

- The ability to continue your endowment regardless of how many moves and the ability to keep the term of the mortgages to 25 years.
- Option to build in financial protection in the form of waiver or critical illness.
- Low start options
- Early redemption option
- The potential of a tax free lump sum

**Disadvantages**

No guarantee that the mortgage will be repaid at end of term. The return is reliant on the investment of the relevant company. Endowments have been receiving a bad press in the last few years as many were miss sold policies and have found themselves in a position where the endowment has not performed well enough to provide enough capital to pay off the mortgage. Take very good advice indeed as to the nature of a particular endowment before entering into a deal.

**Individual Savings Account mortgages**

Once again, with this particular type of mortgage, you pay interest back to the lender and a premium to an insurance company or investment house. The premium is invested and hopefully at the end of the mortgage term the mortgage is repaid from the proceeds of the ISA.

**Advantages of an ISA mortgage**

- Tax efficiency
- Portable
- Can be used as a savings plan

## Disadvantages

- No guarantee
- Can have extra cost of life cover
- No Waver of premium or critical illness allowed in ISA plan
- Limit of what can be invested

## Pension Mortgages

The pension market is without doubt one of the most complicated areas of the financial services industry.

Pension mortgages are mainly targeted at people who are not able to take advantage of an occupational pension scheme and those who are self employed. Pension mortgages can be offered to people who are employed but it is generally considered best advice to take advantage of the company pension scheme therefore making a pension mortgage an unlikely option.

## Considerations

The mortgage cannot represent any more than 25% of the total pension fund at the expected retirement age. The reason for this is that on maturity the maximum cash sum available from the pension is 25% of the fund and the remainder is to provide a pension.

If you are likely to consider the advantages of a pension mortgage you must be able to protect your likely future income and job career prospects as you will be expected to maintain a high level of pension contributions throughout the mortgage term.

To protect the mortgage debt, you will be expected to take out term assurance in order to secure the loan amount for the benefit of the lender.

If you expect your career to change from self-employed to employed with the prospect of a company pension it is generally considered that a pension mortgage would not be suitable for your future requirements.

**Advantages of a pension mortgage**

- Provides a pension and repays mortgage.
- Tax relief on contributions.
- The pension fund is non-taxable.

**Disadvantages**

- Early retirement option purely dependent on the performance of the pension fund.
- A pension mortgage would normally be more expensive than a standard repayment or an endowment mortgage.
- A great deal of the pension is in order to pay off the mortgage .

A pension cannot be in joint names.

**Interest only mortgages**

An interest only mortgage can be compared to having an endowment mortgage without the endowment. Quite simply, the capital will not increase or decrease provided interest payments are maintained. This type of loan is often used for short-term finance or in special cases where individuals cannot afford to cover the costs of capital and interest mortgage.

**Advantages of interest only mortgages**

- Cheap mortgage.

- This method is quite often used by pensioners who want to release capital from their homes to provide them with a lump sum.

## Disadvantages

- The term could be endless. The debt never reduces unless paid off.

**Associated costs of buying a property**

It is important to establish the likely expenditure you will be expected to make before completion of a transaction.

Before a bank or building society will make you an offer they will insist on carrying out a valuation of the proposed property to ensure the property represents adequate security for them to be able to advance you the mortgage monies. The valuation or survey is paid by you and the cost differs from lender to lender. There is also a choice of what type of report you can have carried out in addition to the basic valuation.

Listed below is a general idea of the costs for the various surveys for the purchase of a house costing £275,000:

Valuation for mortgage purposes - £275
Report on condition and valuation - £480
Structural Survey - £500

From time to time a number of mortgage lenders offer free valuations when you apply for a mortgage through them. If you are considering a fixed rate mortgage you will normally be expected to pay a fee. This fee will range from £50-£395 and is paid in most cases on application. Before paying this fee you should find out whether this money is refundable should the transaction not proceed, as in most cases the lender will not return payment.

**Mortgage indemnity or guarantee premium**

Whenever banks or building societies lend more than 75% of the value of the property they insure themselves in the event of future loss in the form of mortgage indemnity. This policy is purely for the benefit of the lender, the premium however is payable by you the applicant. The bigger the deposit you can put down the less indemnity you will pay. Some lenders will allow you to add the indemnity to the mortgage.

Please note that some lenders now pay the MIGP for purchasers up to 90% loan to value and some lenders pay the MIGP up to 95%.

**Solicitors' fees**

A solicitor has to be appointed to act on your behalf and also of the relevant lender. All lenders have a panel of acceptable solicitors and you should check to make sure that you are using a firm that is acceptable otherwise you could be expected to pay two sets of fees.

Your solicitor will carry out various checks and searches and will make numerous enquiries with the owner's solicitors about any issues you or the lender may need to have clarified before you commit yourself.

Based on a purchase price of £275,000 the fees payable to your solicitor would be approximately: £2000 approx plus vat inclusive of disbursements.

**Illustration of Solicitors' Fees and Disbursements**

Purchase price £275,000

Legal fees:

Solicitors £400 + vat

Stamp Duty £1200
Local Authority search fee £90 approx.
Land Registry fee £140 approx.
Land Registry search fee £5
Bankruptcy search fee £1 per client
Other searches such as contamination and water and sewerage etc £200

The most important part of the initial cost is, of course, the deposit money. You will normally be expected to provide at least 5% deposit. This money must be from your own savings or a gift from family etc. because if you are borrowing the money it is effectively a 100% loan. The deposit money is paid to your solicitor on exchange of contracts as this is the time of the transaction when you totally commit yourself to the property. You would normally move in two or three weeks after.

# 3
# Buying and Selling Your Home

## Buying

Once you have established how much you can afford, you will need to approach a number of Estate Agents local to the area in which you wish to buy. They will provide you with a selection of properties within your price range and available for sale. Estate agents will not charge you, the purchaser, a fee, as they earn their money from the vendor (i.e. the person selling the property).

Once you have found a property you like, the normal procedure is to put an offer forward via the estate agent dealing with the property. Remember that he is acting on behalf of the vendor and is duty bound to achieve the best price possible. The best way to approach the negotiations is to inform the estate agent of necessary facts only and of the maximum price you are prepared to pay.

If the vendor agrees to your offer, the next stage is to make a mortgage application and to instruct a solicitor. Once you have received your mortgage offer and your solicitor has all the relevant paperwork, you are in a position to exchange contracts, which means you are committing yourself to the transaction and can only pull out at great expense to yourself.

Normally when you exchange, you pay a deposit of between 5-10% of the purchase price and in some cases, the solicitors' fees. The transaction is normally completed 2-4 weeks after exchange of contracts and you are then at liberty to move into your new home.

## Selling

If you have decided to sell, you can attempt to sell your property privately or use the services of an estate agent.

In today's depressed housing market, the most successful method is via an estate agent. They will normally charge you a percentage of the sale price and if they are not successful in arranging a sale there is no fee. Commissions range from 1.5% + VAT for sole agents to anything up to 3.5% + VAT for multiple agency which means you can instruct more than one agent to market your property. In order to sell your property it may help to have a board outside and a good agent will advertise your property in a local paper. You may find that a small independent agent may offer cheaper fees and greater advertising exposure.

Once a firm offer has been approved by you, it is then a question of waiting for your buyer to get his/her finances through and you can instruct your solicitor to handle the sale and possibly a new purchase for you if you intend to buy again. If you are buying again, it is best to secure a buyer on your own property first otherwise you may get very disappointed if you find a property you want but cannot sell your own. By doing this you will also avoid unnecessary expense.

Any profits made from the sale will be forwarded on to you once your solicitor has deducted all the relevant fees (estate agents' and his own).

## Summary

- Choose an established company with a good reputation.
- If selling, make sure the fees are confirmed in writing.
- If selling, enquire how your property will be marketed (local papers, etc).

# 4
# Life Insurance

The concept of life insurance is by no means a 20th century development. The earliest forms can be traced back to Greek and Roman times. Clubs would be formed and, for a regular contribution, a lump sum would be paid in the event of death of an individual.

In today's society, we are expected to insure for virtually everything and anything and at the end of the month there are normally limited funds to insure for the most important issue, YOU.

**Do you need it?**

Many people feel they do not need life insurance. In some cases this is true but the vast majority have families and feel that they need to be protected in the event of an unexpected death. It is not always the main income provider who needs all the life cover. Provisions must be made if there are children and the non-working parent spends his or her time looking after them. The cost of employing a child minder or even giving up your full time job must be considered. This could be easily remedied with a basic life insurance policy.

If you have a mortgage the banks and building societies normally insist that you have the relevant life insurance to cover the mortgage debt and in the case of endowment mortgages the life insurance forms part of your endowment premiums, but with repayment mortgages the cost of premiums is extra.

As you are probably aware, if you haven't got any life cover other than in conjunction with your mortgage then you are likely to be under-insured.

If you are in an occupational pension scheme you are likely to have cover as part of your benefits. This would normally work out to be 3 times your basic salary and if you have a personal pension plan you can have life cover up to 3 times and you would receive tax relief on your premiums.

To establish how much life cover you require you need to calculate how much income the family needs to survive each year. Take away any state benefits you would be or are entitled to and then multiply this figure by the number of years your youngest child has before he or she leaves school.

### Example

A family requires £15,000 per year income.
No benefits available.
The youngest child is 9. Therefore there is a minimum of 7 years before the child could leave school and start work.
7 x 15 = £105,000 life cover

You could say that the life cover quoted would be too much after the first year, but the youngest child could always go on to sixth form or college and may not actually start work until he or she is 20 years old.

### Different types of life insurance

Most forms of life insurance are paid on a monthly or yearly premium basis. The premium you pay will purchase a level of cover and it can be on a fixed or variable term. There are a multitude of insurance policies geared to the individual's needs and requirements, and we will now look at the differences.

### Decreasing Term Assurance

This policy is commonly known as mortgage protection and is normally used in conjunction with a repayment mortgage. As we have already discovered with a repayment mortgage the debt reduces further throughout the term and the same can be said about the decreasing term insurance. The amount of life cover will decrease in line with the mortgage. This policy can be written in joint names and is the cheapest form of life assurance available. There is no investment value to this contract and in the event of a claim, the benefits are payable to the estate.

## Example

**Mortgage Protection Assurance**
Male non-smoker age at entry not exceeding 30
Female non-smoker age at entry not exceeding 30

*Benefits*

| | |
|---|---|
| Initial sum assured | £50,000 |
| Plan Term | 25 years |

*Monthly cost*
Premium payable for 25 years
or until first death if earlier £9.57

Warning - the contract has no cash-in value at any time.

**Level term insurance**
This policy works on the same basis as the above, but the life cover will not reduce as the term goes on. For this reason, the premiums are slightly more expensive.

**Family income benefit policy**
This policy will simply provide an annual income for your dependents instead of a lump sum. This is a good way too ensure that the provisions that you have made are not used up in one spending spree.

Once again, this contract can be written in joint names, but has no investment value.

### Whole life

This type of policy is considered to be the most flexible contract in the life insurance market. Unlike the other contracts this policy does have investment value and it is not written on a fixed term. The amount of cover you require can be altered at any time to suit changes in your personal circumstances. The premiums you pay are not fixed and are reviewed every 5-10 years to establish whether the insurance cover can still offer you the level of cover for the premium you are paying.

This policy is quite expensive in comparison to term policies. It is, however a great deal more flexible and it can be written in joint names.

**Example**

**Whole of Life min/max cover basis**

Male, non-smoker, age 30 next birthday

Female, non-smoker, age 30 next birthday

Amount of Life Cover payable on first death:

minimum £10,350

maximum £114,900

Monthly premium £25

### Critical illness

A new innovation in the insurance industry is the introduction of critical illness insurance.

Surveys have shown that more people are concerned about being diagnosed as having a critical illness than they are of dying. The implications of having a major illness are immense as you could find yourself stuck with the financial commitments but without the income and ability to pay them.

The introduction of critical illness means that if you are diagnosed with any of the defined illnesses in the contract, you will receive a lump sum. The amount of the lump sum depends on your premiums and your age. The benefit of critical illness means that you can afford private medical treatment or afford to pay off your debts.

Below are listed the main conditions that are considered to be critical illness:

-multiple Sclerosis
-heart Attack
-kidney failure
-loss of a limb
-stroke
-major organ transplant
-cancer
-Coma
-benign brain tumour
-severe burns

This is not a technical guide or a total list of definitions. It is simply a selection of some definitions.

Critical illness can be taken out by itself, or as part of a whole life or endowment. Critical illness does not have investment value. It can be written in joint names.

**Example**

Male, non-smoker, age next 30 next birthday
Female, non-smoker, age 30 next birthday

Initial monthly premium £25.00
Initial sum assured £65,000
Life Assured basis joint life, first event
Cover type Maximum

The premium is payable until the earlier of the:
- death of the last to die of the lives assured.
- diagnosis of one of the lives assured suffering a critical illness.

The premium will increase annually by the amount required to support the increase in benefits as a result of the Automatic Increase Option.

**What the benefits might be**

The greater of the sum assured and the encashment value of the plan will be payable on the diagnosis of one of the lives assured suffering a critical illness.

Warning - the contract has no cash-in value at any time.

# 5
# Savings

People save for a number of different reasons, dependent on their circumstances and on age. Some people save in order to have enough to help their children and others save for a prosperous old age. Whatever the reason, it is important to understand the best vehicles for savings

Those skilled in the art of financial planning consider that a sum of between three and six months expenditure constitutes an adequate fund for emergencies. This will depend on your employment status as if you are self-employed then you may need more due to the fact that you will not get sick pay unless you are insured.

This emergency cash should be placed in an account that is readily accessible, probably in an instant access account which allows you to withdraw without penalty. However, these accounts traditionally pay the lowest form of interest and it is advisable to shop around.

There are a number of newer accounts, such as telephone only accounts which offer a higher rate of interest with instant access. You are provided with a card so that you can gain access to your money as and when you need it. If the account is joint, then both partners should be provided with a card. In addition to phone accounts there are internet accounts. Although some of the providers are large established institutions such as Northern Rock and Abbey National, some are smaller companies with far less capital. You should always think before investing with any company. Think about your needs and requirements and the security of your capital.

## Cash returns

A lot of savers like to have more cash on deposit than they need for emergencies. If you do not need access to the money for emergencies then it is better to put your money in a higher rate account, one which generally needs notice of withdrawal. The longer the period of notice the more interest that you will get on your money.

Postal accounts also pay higher than standard rates of interest and these are useful for those savers who do not require access to their savings over a foreseeable period.

You can get an idea of interest rates by perusing the pages of the dailies and weekend editions of papers, which compare the costs of borrowing and returns on savings. In the United Kingdom rates for deposits are usually quoted gross of tax. Rates may be quotes on two different bases.

The nominal rate is the rate of interest applied to the account, while the annual effective rate (AER) is the rate taking into account the frequency of interest payments.

The nominal rate is not affected by whether you draw your interest or leave it in the account. But if interest is paid more than once a year and you leave it there, you will earn interest in interest and end the year with more in your account.

The table below shows the difference between the nominal and effective rates depending on how often interest is credited to your account.

If you plan to spend all your interest, you can compare different accounts on the basis of their nominal interest rates. If you plan to leave the interest to accumulate, as the table shows, an account with a lower nominal interest rate could give you a better deal if it is credited more frequently. In this case, you should use the annual effective rate as a comparison.

## Annual effective rate if interest is credited

| Nominal rate | Yearly | Half-yearly | Quarterly | Monthly | Daily |
|---|---|---|---|---|---|
| 5% | 5% | 5% | 5.09 | 5.12% | 5.13% |
| 8% | 8% | 8.16% | 8.24% | 8.30% | 8.33% |

## Tax on interest earned

Tax is usually deducted at source in interest paid. This is a requirement of the effective legislation. Tax is deducted at 20%. If you pay a lesser rate of tax then you can reclaim overpaid tax. To have interest on savings paid without deduction of tax, the account holder has to sign a form R85 declaring that they are a non-taxpayer. Parents can sign this on behalf of children. If the interest paid to a child from money given to it by parents is over £10 then this will be taxed as if this were the parent's income.

Banks based outside the UK, i.e. offshore are not subject to UK tax legislation and many of these institutions offer interest gross. Whether you receive it gross or not you are still obliged by law to declare it on your tax return. It is the savers responsibility to declare the tax.

Some National Savings accounts pay interest gross and this is subject to the same rules. I.e. the taxpayer declaring the interest received.

## The choice of accounts

There are a wide variety of accounts available from banks and building societies. Many accounts have differing features. Most pay variable interest but some pay fixed rates. The following are some of the accounts on offer.

### Children's accounts

These accounts sometimes offer better variable rates than can be gained on a small deposit on a regular savings account. These accounts can also offer free gifts for children, such as magazines, moneyboxes etc.

### Instant access accounts

These permit withdrawal of capital without notice, though there is usually a restriction on how much cash can be withdrawn on one day. The interest rate is variable. Interest may be credited yearly, half yearly, quarterly, monthly or daily. With most accounts, the rate will depend on the amount invested.

### Internet accounts

These accounts can only be set up over the internet. The initial transfer is made from your current account, as are future transfers. Interest rates are usually higher than traditional accounts.

### Mini-Isas

The individual savings account takes two forms, the mini-isas and the maxi-isas. A mini-isa can contain cash, equities (stocks and shares) or insurance, while a maxi-isa can contain all three elements.

You can take out a mini-isa of each kind each year or a single maxi-isa, but you cannot invest in both in a single tax year. You can invest up to £3000 per year until 5th April 2006, and these isas are tax-free.

The maximum for a maxi-isa is £7000 in a single tax year.

These rules are subject to change so you should check with your bank or building society.

**Monthly income accounts**
These types of accounts may have a minimum notice period for withdrawal. The income is usually paid direct to your current account and there is usually a £250 minimum amount.

**Notice accounts**
Money can be withdrawn without penalty by giving the appropriate amount of notice. If you withdraw without notice you will lose interest on the amount you would have been paid during the notice period. There is usually a minimum deposit of £1000 or more.

**Postal accounts**
Some building societies offer these accounts, where deposits and withdrawals can only be made by post. Interest rates are variable and may be higher than on instant access accounts, as are the minimum investments required.

**Telephone accounts**
The initial deposit is made by cheque. You set up a direct debit arrangement on your current account and can then transfer money between it and your telephone account. You have to set up a security code and cite this when calling to transact business. Interest rates are usually very competitive.

**Time deposits**
The interest rate is fixed for the time of the deposit, often 30 days onwards. There will be a penalty for early withdrawal. Interest is usually added at the end of the period that is fixed and is usually gross of tax.

## Fixed-rate investments

You can commit your money for a fixed period; say five years, at a certain rate of interest, say 6%. If rates are at 4% this may seem attractive but rates can rise during the period. Before investing for the longer term at fixed rates you should consider carefully the market in the longer term and decide whether you want to make this gamble. Fixed interest rates will offer you a reasonable return over the period and it is difficult to predict interest rates over the longer term.

## Short-term fixed-rate investments

### Escalator bonds

These are issued by building societies and pay a rate of interest that rises each year for a fixed period. Since these are fixed rate accounts you cannot get it back early or there can be a significant financial penalty. You should always think about the consequences of your wish to invest in this type of product.

### Fixed rate bonds

These accounts pay a flat fixed rate of interest for a fixed period from one to five years. Early withdrawal is not usually permitted without a penalty. There will be a minimum investment.

### Guaranteed growth bonds

Issued by insurance companies, these guarantee a fixed rate for a specified period, usually between two and five years. A lump sum is paid at the end of the term. The return is treated as having borne basic rate tax so there will only be an additional liability if you are a higher rate taxpayer.

### Guaranteed income bonds

These pay a fixed income for a specified term, usually two to five years. The tax treatment is the same as for the above bonds.

**Maxi-isas**
Some companies offer maxi-isas for a fixed rate of return for periods of up to five years. Sometimes a rate of income is guaranteed but you may not get all your capital back unless a stock market index (FTSE100 usually) is above a certain level. These are higher-risk so careful thought needs to go into investments such as this.

**National Savings Certificates**
These grow in value at a fixed rate for a period of up to five years. The profits are exempt from tax and there are limits on how much you can invest.

**National Savings Pensioners Guaranteed Bonds**
These pay a fixed amount of income over two to five years. The interest is taxable but is paid without deduction at source.

**Longer-term savings plans**
**Isa savings plans**
Maxi-isas, in which you may invest or save up to £7000 each tax year up to 5th April 2006, are well suited to regular savers. They are exempt from income tax and capital gains tax. They give access to a range of investment funds and offer flexibility. Minimum savings are usually £50-100 per month. There is a cost of between 1% and 5% of each contribution within the year plus an annual charge on the assets of the fund of between 0.5% and 2%. Look at the charges carefully. Isas must be in the name of one individual. You cannot take out a maxi-isa in a child's name.

**Unit trust savings plans**
Unit trusts and open-ended investment companies are similar in having a pool of money which they manage on behalf of individual and corporate investors. The pool expands or contracts

depending on the additions or withdrawals into it and the value of a unit or share is the value of the investments in the pool divided by the number of units or shares in issue.

A wide variety of funds are available, investing in a variety of areas and countries. Minimum monthly savings are from £30-£50. The income received is taxable and will usually be taxed at source. Higher rate taxpayers will receive a certificate showing what they have paid at source and they will be personally responsible for any extra payments. Costs vary from 1%-5% of each contribution with an annual charge of 0.5% to 2% of the value of your assets. You can take out a plan in the name of a child.

## Investment trusts

Unlike unit trusts or open-ended investment companies, investment trusts do not issue new shares to savers but buy existing shares through the stock market. This is because investment trusts have a fixed pool of assets and the price of a share in the market may be higher or lower than its net asset value. These schemes are rum by investment trust managers. They usually subsidise the costs of the plan, which are much lower than the costs of buying investment trust shares through a stockbroker. The annual charges are between 0.5% and 2%. The taxation rules and child rules are the same as for unit trusts.

## With profits savings plans

With profits savings plans are in the form of endowment polices issued by insurance companies. Though they are life policies, they provide very little life cover. Most of the premiums that are paid are used to invest in the companies with profits fund, which is a giant pool of assets usually worth billions of pounds. The fund will hold a variety of assets including fixed rate investments, UK and overseas shares and property.

The with-profits policy has a sum assured, which is the minimum amount that is paid on death or at the maturity rate. Two types of bonus are added to the sum assured. Reversionary bonuses are added each year, often at quite a lower rate of 3% or so. At maturity (or death) a terminal bonus is added which can be equal to al the reversionary bonuses paid. Once a reversionary bonus has been added to a policy, it cannot be taken away, but terminal bonus rates are not guaranteed and can be varied at any time.

With-profits policies are of two types. Some have one fixed maturity date, while with a 'flexible policy' you can en-cash it at several different dates, usually at five-year intervals. The charges for with profits policies are typically about 12-15% of premiums over the term.

The term for these policies is usually quite long, being anything from 10-25 years so careful thought needs to be given to this type of investment. They are only really suitable if you can sustain your savings over this long period.

## Friendly society plans

Friendly societies are permitted to run tax-free savings schemes with low minimum and maximum investments. Some are of the with-profit types, while others are unit-linked. The plans have a minimum term of ten years and the high costs can wipe out other benefits so again careful thought has to be given to this type of investment.

## The purpose of saving

The purposes of saving, as we have seen, are many and will differ depending on your circumstances and long-term view. Some of the more usual savings objectives are to provide retirement income, to pay for children's education (see later) to reduce debt such as mortgage and for general purposes, for life's little luxuries.

Whatever you choose, you should do so carefully, think about the short and long-term advantages and don't take unnecessary risks.

# 6
# Single Premium and Lump Sum Investments

---

If you are able to consider investing a lump sum of money, you must take great care in establishing your requirements for that investment and also your own future plans. For example:

-you may not be worried about getting a significant return as long as it is likely to better the return you would get from your building society account;

-you need the best return possible over the next five years without jeopardizing capital;

-you aren't worried how the money is invested provided you don't receive a tax bill;

Quite clearly, the important issues to remember when investing a lump sum are:

1. the amount of money you can afford to invest;
2. the term of the investment;
3. the risk involved with the investment;
4. tax implications.

As we have already seen in the regular savings chapter, there are numerous ways in which you can invest your money and the same considerations should be made whether you are saving on a regular basis or a lump sum.

considerations should be made whether you are saving on a regular basis or a lump sum.

## The options available

Your choice of investment will obviously depend on your own personal financial circumstances. Below you will find details of the most popular investments currently available.

## High interest building society accounts

If you are concerned about the risk attached with investing your money, then you cannot do a lot better than your building society. Although some people may consider investing in their building society as unattractive, you haven't got any worries about how your money is being invested. For lump sums, building societies often offer a wide range of higher rate accounts with a tiered rate of interest, depending on the size of investment. Most high rate accounts have a notice period which must be given for any withdrawals. This may not apply, however, if the balance of the account remains over £5,000. A large number of high rate accounts will allow you to take a regular income on a monthly basis. The interest received on these accounts has already been taxed at a composite rate and should you be a high rate tax-payer, you may have a tax liability on the interest.

## National savings

Most national savings are calculated gross and therefore you would have a tax liability if you are a tax payer, therefore reducing the benefit of investing. There are however, a limited number of savings opportunities that deserve a mention.

## Ordinary accounts

This is a basic account which will allow you to invest between £10-£10,000. The interest rate increases for amounts in excess of

£500. This is a good investment for higher rate tax-payers as the first £70 interest is non-taxable.

## Savings certificates

This is a good way of investing your money over a five-year period especially if interest rates are high. The interest you will receive is fixed and tax-free and you can invest a maximum of £10,000 or £20,000 if you re-invest after the first five years.

## Indexed linked certificates

These certificates are based on the rate of inflation and on the five- year term of the savings certificates. If inflation looks like it is going to constantly increase, this is a very attractive investment for minimum risk as you will receive a tax-free bonus after 5 years.

## Investment bonds

Investment bonds are considered a medium to long-term investment and the investment options range from the with profits investments to investments in the property markets and overseas. The risk is always a major factor in any investment and you should be aware exactly where your money is being invested and the relative risk.

All major insurance companies offer investment bonds and they can be used for both capital growth and income if required. The investment fund is taxable and payments are made net of basic rate tax. There is an allowance however, which will allow both basic rate and higher rate taxpayers to withdraw up to 5% of the fund value each year without liability.

The minimum amount that you can invest in a bond is normally £2,000 and you should consider investing it for a minimum of five years. In the case of an emergency, you would be able to gain access to your money but the value will relate to the period of investment, charges and market conditions.

The main points to remember are that you should invest in a bond that suits your attitude to risk. If you are a higher rate taxpayer you may be able to reduce any liability if you can cash in the bond when the income drops to the basic rate bracket.

## Guaranteed Capital Investments

This is a relatively new concept in the insurance industry as your investment is directly linked to the performance of the FTSE one hundred. If you read the financial press or watch the main television news you will always see a reference to the FTSE one hundred. It provides a clear indication of how the stock market is behaving as it monitors the share prices of the top 100 companies in the UK.

From day to day the prices of each company's shares can change for any reason and towards the bottom of the index the smaller companies are constantly competing to secure their position within the top 100.

The growth of the FTSE is often compared to that of banks and building societies (see single premium investments) and over a long term period is considered to be a valuable alternative to the standard options. Traditionally, the FTSE has outperformed the returns offered by building society accounts and for that reason most insurance companies will guarantee that on completion of the five year term you will at least receive your original investment, thereby reducing the risk factor.

The minimum investment is usually £6,000 and the fund and benefits are paid net of basic rate tax. Guaranteed capital investments are offered on limited availability and are not able to provide an income. They are, however, a worthwhile consideration when you are building up an investment portfolio.

## Unit Trusts

The purpose of the unit trust is to give individuals the opportunity to invest directly in the stock market. There are a multitude of investment opportunities ranging from UK equities to shares in Japan and North America. In order to overcome the charges and realise a profit, you must look at investing your money in a unit trust for at least three years or longer.

Unit trusts can be used for capital growth or income and you should obtain help from a financial advisor to choose the most suitable trust for your performance. Once you have chosen your trust and paid your money, you will be issued with a certificate. It is very important that you keep this in a safe place as you will need to produce it when you cash it in.

To establish how well your investment is doing, you can phone the trust managers or look at the share page of any quality newspaper. You will normally see two columns, the offer price and the bid price. For the purpose of selling you must multiply the bid price by the number of units you hold.

## The tax implications

Unless you are a higher rate tax-payer it is unlikely that you will have any tax liability on the income or gain of the investment. If you are a higher rate tax-payer there are various ways of mitigating your liability and you should discuss this with a financial advisor before committing yourself to any investment.

## Individual Savings Accounts

We have already looked at ISA's in depth. ISA's, as they are known have been made available since April 5th 1999 when PEP's and TESSA's were withdrawn. Refer to pages 50-51 for a detailed breakdown of ISA's.

# 7
# Income Protection

We all realise the importance of life insurance. We do however mainly neglect the need to ensure that there is adequate protection to cover accidents or illness that prevent us from working and therefore maintaining our normal standard of living.

Most employers restrict the length of time that they will make full payment to the employee in the event of illness and the self employed are likely to receive even less.

To protect against accident or sickness, you can take out an income protection plan. For a monthly premium you can cover a pre-determined amount of money relative to a maximum two thirds of your income. The premium you will pay will depend on:

1. How much benefit you require;
2. Your age;
3. How long you are prepared to wait before you receive benefits (deferment period 4 weeks - one year);
4. Your medical condition;
5. Your occupation.

If you make a claim on your income protection policy, the benefits will be paid to you until such time as you are able to return to your normal job or one of a similar nature, or your expected retirement date. This type of cover will not protect you against redundancy.

In the event of a claim, the benefits you receive represent and replace your income and therefore attract tax at the relevant rate.

## Cover offered by banks and building societies

The threat of losing your job is common in today's society and it is something that could ruin your lifestyle and bring great hardship to you and your family.

The banks and building societies are of course aware of this and therefore offer you the opportunity to apply for a scheme which will protect you and your partner (in the case of a joint mortgage) against accident or sickness or involuntary redundancy. This is sometimes referred to as mortgage payment protection or payment care.

The premiums for these types of schemes range from £6 per £100 of cover to £9 per £100. A claim can only be made and benefits paid once you have been unable to work for a period of three months, after which stage the benefits are normally paid for a period of one to two years for sickness and also for redundancy. Some insurers when paying benefit will send a cheque direct to your lender each month to ensure you are using the money for the purpose that was intended.

These schemes have proved very popular and you should seek further information about them from the relevant lender, as you are not likely to be given a chance to take out a policy after your mortgage has been completed.

You can also allow for extra benefit from these policies to cover the cost of any endowments or life insurances that may run in conjunction with the mortgage.

This type of cover is of benefit to the employed but the redundancy cover is obviously of no benefit to the self-employed and a good permanent health insurance would be more relevant. If the benefits of the scheme are paid direct to you, that would constitute income and income tax would be payable at the relevant rate.

# 8
# Pensions

A pension is designed to replace a regular income you would normally receive from your job. When you retire you are given the option of taking a lump sum and a reduced pension or just a pension.

Thanks to better working conditions and advances in medicine, the average life expectancy has significantly increased within the last 30 years and therefore the importance of adequate pension provisions has been made more apparent to us all.

Although most people are eligible for the state pension, this in itself does not provide the income necessary to maintain the standard of living you may be accustomed to. The government actively encourages people to make their own pension arrangements as they can see the number of people claiming state benefits steadily increasing putting great strain on the state system.

Only relatively recently, the state retirement date for females born after 1955 was increased to 65, the same as men. If the average life expectancy is to increase much further, the government may consider moving the goalposts once again.

The purpose of this chapter is to inform you of the various types of schemes and what you can do to improve your benefits when you retire.

## The state pension

To qualify for a state pension you must have been paid or credited with National Insurance contributions for 90% of your working life. Provided you have contributed 25% of this time you will receive a reduced pension.

You will receive credits if:

-you are claiming maternity, sickness, invalidity or unemployment benefit;
-you are male aged 60-64 not working;
-you are in full time education;
-you are on an approved training course or at home looking after the elderly or children.

You should check with the Department of Work and Pensions to ascertain the current level of pension.

**The State Earnings related Pension Scheme (SERPS)**
SERPS was introduced by the Government in the late 1970s to provide additional retirement benefits to boost the state pension. A proportion of the National Insurance represented the SERPS element. It was not, however, invested for your own benefit but simply redirected to other people who were receiving pension benefits. Your own pension will be funded by the contributions of the next generation of workers. Needless to say, if pensioners outnumber workers then this system will soon become bankrupt and with this in mind the Government altered the rules on SERPS and reduced the benefits within the scheme and in 1988 encouraged people to opt out of SERPS so that their own National Insurance contributions were directly invested into their own pension scheme.

**Personal Pension for the self-employed**
If you are self-employed you will only receive a basic state pension and therefore it is vital that you make the appropriate arrangements to maintain the standard of living you are used to. There is the added advantage that the contributions you make towards your pension are eligible for tax relief and as with all

pensions the money is invested in a tax free fund and at your own desired retirement date after the age of 50, you can take part of your pension benefits as a tax free lump sum. The amount of money you can invest in your pension per year is very generous and the older you get, the more you can contribute.

**Contribution limits to personal pension plans**
**Age on 6th April -% of net relevant earnings**

| | |
|---|---|
| Up to 35 | 17.5 |
| 36-45 | 20 |
| 46-50 | 25 |
| 51-55 | 30 |
| 56-60 | 35 |
| 61-74 | 40 |

If you find you are able to put a lump sum into a pension, you can do so provided it does not exceed your contributions limit. If you have exceeded your limit, you are able to go back up to 6 years to claim your allowance for the years you haven't paid maximum contributions.

As part of your personal pension plan, you can have a number of additional benefits:

1. **Life cover**: you can have life cover for 3 times your net income and receive tax relief on your contributions;
2. **Waiver of premium**: in the event of an illness or accident making it impossible to work then the waiver benefit would maintain your pension premiums 6 months after your claim and until you were able to return to work;
3. **Indexation**: The cost of living generally increases each year. In order to combat this, your pension contributions can be altered

each year in line with market changes and therefore keep your contributions to a realistic level.

With any pension, the earlier you are able to start contributing the greater the benefits will be at retirement. The minimum age for someone wanting to take out a pension is 16 and the benefits can be taken between 50-75 years old.

Similar to endowments, your pension contributions are invested in a range of different funds but the investment grows completely free of any tax, therefore allowing the potential of significantly greater growth and returns.

**Personal pension for the employed**

If you are employed by the civil service, local government or any major corporation, the likelihood is that you will have the opportunity to join the company pension scheme. In most cases it would be beneficial to do so for the simple reason that the employer would normally make a contribution to your pension as well, which is usually considerable, as well as your own contribution which is taken from your own salary.

Smaller companies quite often don't offer their employees a group scheme and therefore it is down to the individual to make his or her own arrangements.

The pension for an employed person is similar to a self employed person with the exception that the tax relief for an employed person is calculated every month.

The employed person also has the option of contracting out of SERPS and redirecting his or her National Insurance contributions into the personal pension plan. Before you do this you should seek financial advice.

The benefit of having a Personal Pension Plan if you are employed is that if you decide to change jobs you can take the pension with you and the benefits will not be affected.

Premiums can be stopped for a period of time and resumed at a later stage and if you are offered the opportunity to join a company pension scheme then you could suspend your own plan or possibly transfer it to a free standing additional voluntary contribution if you wish to continue the plan.

## Occupational Pension Schemes

### Final salary

This type of occupational pension is designed to provide remuneration at pensionable age relative to your final year's salary. The benefits are calculated based on length of pensionable service and salary.

### Money Purchase Schemes

A money purchase scheme is based on your contributions to the pension fund and rate of return it has managed to achieve. At retirement age the accumulated fund is released to purchase an annuity which is designed to provide the necessary pension income. The disadvantage of the annuity however is that it is dependent on the prevailing interest in order to offer attractive rates of return.

### Non-Contributory Pension Schemes

Some people are fortunate to be working for employers who offer non-contributory schemes. This is effectively a free pension scheme and without doubt a most valuable benefit.

### Free standing additional voluntary contributions

If you are employed and unlikely to receive the maximum pension benefits when you retire, you can consider the benefits of AVCs. An AVC was designed to boost the pension benefits of individuals who have limited pensionable service (average pensionable service, 30 years). Unlike a pension, an AVC will not give you an option to take a lump sum. It does however, have exactly the same tax relief benefits. AVCs are normally targeted at people in their late 40's who have worked for various employers and are currently part of a company pension scheme with limited previous pension provisions.

**Pension transfers**

If you have been part of an occupational pension scheme and left the service of that employer, you are sent a statement of benefits shortly after your departure. The statement will advise you of the accrued benefits to date and the likely benefits at the known retirement date.

At this stage you are given two options:

Option 1 is to leave your pension with the employer and to take the benefits when you retire.

Option 2 is to transfer the benefits into a personal pension plan so that you can have direct control of the fund and possible future contributions.

There are many arguments for and against pension transfers and you must analyze the two options on a like-for-like basis before making any decisions.

Anyone who is currently in a pension scheme at work, and intends to remain with that employer is normally best advised to stay in that scheme and not make alternative provisions. The pensions market is very flexible and therefore you must consider carefully your long-term career plans to make the most appropriate and beneficial pension provisions.

# 9
# Stocks and shares

Successful investing through the stock market can provide very high returns. However, the stock market can also lose you a lot of money, especially in the current climate. As an individual investor in shares, the costs of investing will be your biggest handicap. You might pay commission of about 1% to buy or sell a share if you deal on an 'execution only' basis. This is many times what a large institution will pay-simply because larger institutions deal in large amounts.

## Today's stock market

The nature and form of the stock market has been changing for decades. Many British companies now have share listings in New York as well as London. The major European stock exchanges are talking about mergers. New all-electronic exchanges threaten the older established exchanges in Europe and America.

As far as small and mainly domestically focused companies are concerned, the choice is between a listing on the London Stock Exchange (LSE) a listing on the Alternative Investment market (AIM) or making arrangements for the shares to be traded privately, as they are through Ofex. (See later).

The LSE is more demanding than AIM in terms of its listing requirements and charges higher fees. Companies without track records cannot list on it. The overall checks and audits prior to listing are far more stringent than for an AIM listing.

Ofex is not a market at all, it is simply a facility for trading shares in privately owned companies that have not been subject to an exchanges listing rules. Just because a firm is a Public Limited company (PLC) does not mean it is listed on a stock exchange. It only means that it has more than five shareholders and pays slightly more in audit fees for its annual report than a limited company.

Individuals are not allowed to trade directly on stock exchanges. They must transact their deals through stockbrokers who are accredited members of the exchange. The brokers are responsible for settling transactions, which means collecting and paying over the money. The security and dependency of settlement is another defining feature of developed stock markets, but this is notably absent from emerging stock markets.

When you buy or sell shares, the stockbroker deals with a market maker who buys and sells shares, aiming to make tiny profits on most trades. The market maker will risk his or her own capital doing this, whereas the broker simply acts as your agent.

## Shareholders and shares

Shareholders in a business are the last in line when it comes to entitlement to take money out. A company has legal responsibility for the following:

- Any taxes due to the government including income tax etc
- Any taxes due to a local authority such as business rates
- Wages due to its employees
- Money owed to its bankers
- Payments due to its suppliers
- Money owed to other lenders including bondholders

All the above rank above shareholders. Only when they have been paid is a company entitled to make payments to its shareholders. Shareholders thus bear the most risk. Since they are entitled to everything that is left after a company meets its obligations then the returns can be high if the company prospers.

Companies can make themselves more or less risky for shareholders, The major factor is debt. The more debt a company has the more it has to earn to satisfy shareholders. The ratio of debt to equity is therefore one of the most important features of a company's financing.

Analysing companies accounts used to be a mater of combing through the books but this work can now be done by providers of databases over the internet. However, if you want to understand more then you should read a book on valuing companies so that you have a clearer idea of the principles.

## Recognising a good business

Defining a successful company is difficult. There are two important points for investors to recognise:

- Nothing lasts forever. However good you think a company is, you must keep an eye on its performance. If its standards look as if they are going to slip, investigate quickly and, unless you find good reasons to expect an upturn, then sell
- You saw it first. Good or bad news on the high street is visible in the stores long before city analysts can measure it in sales or profits figures. Empty department stores give you a clue months before the shares crash.

## Trust your experience

There are many areas in which professional full time investors enjoy advantages over individual investors. Professional fund managers spend a large part of their lives investing on behalf of clients and are very knowledgeable indeed. However, an individual also has basic common sense experience which can be applied to the area of buying and selling shares.

## Choosing an investment style

There are many different styles of investing. The word style is appropriate because this is not just about deciding on a method but how to apply it. There are a number of different styles, or approaches, to investing, three of which are listed below.

## Value investing

Value investing is the approach that has been in use for longest and with the most consistent results. Many successful investors, such as Warren Buffet, follow this approach, first fashioned by Benjamin Graham from the 1920's to the 1950's. The key features of value investing are:

- The business. Know and understand the business, its history, its strengths and weaknesses, its management and products and its opportunities.
- The numbers. Value investing is very analytical, in particular, look at trends in terms of sales, profits and earnings. In short, build up a picture of the business for yourself.
- The margin of safety. This was Benjamin Graham's key contribution-he wanted to buy a dollar for sixty cents. In the 20'sand 30's through to the sixties it was easy to do so. If you analysed the numbers many shares on offer at sixty cents were clearly worth a dollar, given the companies assets base. Buying such shares gave a margin of safety that Graham always wanted.
- In more recent times, very few shares have been available on terms like that. This is partly because tangible assets such as land and buildings, important in Grahams day, now make up a small proportion of companies assets. Nowadays the value of a companies brands, patents and personnel is often more important than tangible assets.

Measuring these is nor easy therefore the margin of safety is not easy to deduce.

## Growth investing

When the number of companies whose shares were seen as value investments shrank in the 1950's and 1960's, analysts looked for other methods of investing. One that was very successful indeed was the growth investing style of T Rowe Price, an American stockbroker. He argued that it was worth paying a high price for shares in companies capable of rapid growth in profits and earnings, and the boom of the 1950's and 60's proved him right.

The market crash in 1969-70 saw many growth company shares fall by 50% or more, and for a while this form of investing was marginalized. It re-emerged in the late 1990's as technology related stocks soared in value on the basis of their supposed ability to produce very high rates of growth in earnings for many years.

## The life cycle views

T Rowe Price believed that companies went through a life cycle. In their earliest and latest stages they were most risky. But the least risky time to own them was when they had established themselves and sales and profits were growing strongly. The aim was to own them until they entered the period of maturity and sell them before they entered the period of decadence.

Another view is that of cyclical and secular growth, where the ideal growth stock is one capable of secular growth in earnings, which means that it will continue to grow through several business cycles during which its sector and the whole economy expands and contracts. Shares in companies like this will still fall along with those of its peers in a cyclical downturn, but will recover much more strongly in the next downturn.

Whatever choice you make, the majority of professional investors own the bulk of shares and it is they who determine short-term and even medium-term market movements.

The problem with professional investors is that they are accountable to investors, advisors and trustees on a short-term basis. This motivates them to attain short-term results. This motivates them to attain short-term results. What they tend to do, in broad terms, they pile into sectors and shares they believe will go up in the short term and out of those they consider will go down in the short term. Their timescale is three to six months or at most a year.

This approach can prove fatal, as has been demonstrated by hi-tech stocks, with a lot of money being ploughed into what was perceived as high growth stocks. The result is history with many of those stocks being worthless.

### Stockbroker services

Stockbrokers offer two sorts of dealing services to individual investors: advisory and execution only.

### Advisory

With an advisory service, you may ask your broker for advice. The broker may also provide research material and newsletters. Dealing costs are usually between 1.5% to 1.9% on the value of each trade. You will usually deal with the same individual or group who will get to know you and your account.

### Execution-only

With an execution only service, the broker offers no advice and takes no responsibility for your investment choices. He will simply provide a dealing and settlement service. The cost is usually under 1% of the value of a trade.

Normally, when you call a broker with an order you will not know until sometime later whether you actually got the shares or sold them at a specific price. With newer internet services you can in many cases deal in real time. Effectively, you can get access to the same dealing systems the brokers use, and can confirm your purchase of a number of shares at a specific price at a click of your mouse.

Price competition has already reduced execution only dealing costs significantly in the last few years and is likely to cut them further.

Until recently, when you bought shares, you received a share certificate. This was not legal title of ownership. Legally, it is the entry on the company's share register that represents title to shares, but it was traditional to issue certificates.

Now all trading and settlement is handled electronically, registration of ownership has also gone electronic with larger companies and is moving that way either smaller companies. Stockbrokers prefer you to hold your shares in a nominee account, which means that the broker operates one nominee account through which all clients' shareholdings are held. Instead of a share certificate you receive a statement. You can open your own account with the stock exchange clearing system (crest) but the charges may be as much as £100 per year with many brokers.

## Cutting losses as an individual investor

Most professional investors will agree that individual investors do worse than they could because they do not dump their losers but hold them all the way to the bottom. This is a matter of psychology. If you over-identify with your investments, the failure of one becomes a personal failure

This should not blind you to the reality. This test is one proposed by several professional investors. Regardless of what you paid for it when you bough it, and knowing what you know

now about the company, would you buy its shares at the present price? If not, sell.

### Researching companies

Doing your own research on companies is easier now in the age of the Internet. An increasing number of PLC's have their own websites from which you can download annual reports and other investor information. Stockbrokers are starting to offer free research reports. Many offer access to charts of share prices. Independent sites tell you how many shares are rising and falling. Which company directors are buying and selling, which shares are being bought or sold by private investors. In addition, there is a lot of information available in newspapers and magazines.

### Investment clubs

One way of learning about investing is to join an investment club. Members meet regularly and trade ideas, argue and select shares in which their pooled money (small amounts) is invested. An organisation called proshare provides guidance on setting up a club.

### Finally

Investment, careful investment, takes time. Share investment can be a hobby if you stick to a few simple trading rules and do not over commit yourself. If you want to spend more time and invest more money then you need to be realistic about the amount of time that you need to do this effectively.

Above all, be cautious, know the market, understand something about the principles of investment and make a decision about whether you are looking for short, medium or long term growth.

# 10

# Tax

## Income Tax

Regardless of whether we are employed or self-employed, we all have to accept the fact that the Inland Revenue are going to take a percentage of our income in the form of income tax and there is nothing we can do to avoid it.

The employed and self-employed are treated in slightly different ways and therefore we shall look at each individually, once we have assessed the structure of income tax. You should check your current tax allowances with the Inland Revenue as they are subject to annual change.

## Income Tax Structure

Single person
Tax allowance £6305

The personal allowance shows how much a person can earn before they have to pay any tax. In the case of a married man he can earn an extra £2110 before paying tax. (The married person's allowance, however, can be transferred to the spouse if requested.)

The first £1920 of a persons income is taxable at 10%. The next £27980 is taxed at 22% and all income after that at 40%' (tax year 2002-2003)

The various rates of tax are called the marginal rates.

## The Employed

If you are employed your tax affairs are conducted on the fiscal year or financial year which is 6th April to 5th April the following year.

You are taxed on what is known as Schedule E (Pay As You Earn) which means that both tax and national insurance will be deducted by your employer before you receive your salary cheque. You therefore receive your salary net of tax. This is without doubt the simplest way to conduct your tax affairs as there is very little further communication you need to have, if any, with your tax office.

At the end of the financial year you will receive a P60 which is a statement of your full year's earnings and it will contain details of how much tax and national insurance you have paid as well as pension contributions if you are in an occupational pension scheme.

You should always keep your P60 in a safe place as it often requested by banks and building societies for mortgage or loan purposes.

If you work for a large employer you may receive fringe benefits such as a company car, mortgage subsidy, or private medical insurance. These are very worthwhile benefits but you must remember they are also taxable benefits which will mean that your personal allowance will reduce to account for the real value of these benefits. If you have such benefits but notice your tax code hasn't changed then it is your responsibility to inform your tax office, as failure to do so may mean that in future years they could claim payment for undisclosed benefits.

Not all benefits are taxable, however, and the most attractive one is obviously a company pension scheme. In recent years a great deal of companies have moved towards Performance Related Pay and there is a tax concession which will allow them to pay a bonus known as Profit Related Pay up to a maximum of

£4000 pa without any tax liability regardless of your marginal rate. This is obviously an excellent concession for everyone concerned. Employees who earn less than £8500 receive lenient treatment with regard to the cost of any benefits they receive.

When you leave employment you will be provided with a P45 which is similar to a P60 but is for the benefit of your new employer to use in order to calculate your earnings to date and therefore make the necessary stoppages in your salary. It is always worthwhile taking a copy of your P45 for your own reference.

**The self-employed**

If you are self employed your own tax year can be any period of 12 months you want. In the eyes of the Inland Revenue you will be taxed on what is known as Schedule D and pay Class 2 National Insurance contributions.

Being self employed means that the money you receive for the services you provide will be gross and therefore no tax will have been deducted.

It is advisable that you keep an accurate record of all the money you receive and receipts for any money you spend in connection with your business activities. At the beginning of April you would normally receive a tax return form which explores all the potential sources of income you may have. This must be duly signed and returned within a month.

A large percentage of the self employed use the services of an accountant, as they best know the ways in which your tax liability can be reduced and their services certainly make it easier if you are self-employed and are hoping to take out a mortgage.

The Inland Revenue will negotiate with you or your accountant once they have details of your year's earnings and business expenses. Once the expenses have been taken from the gross figure this will leave your net income and therefore the amount upon which you will be expected to pay tax.

Your tax liability is normally paid in 2 installments, the first on 1st January and the second on the 1st July. The Inland Revenue, however, do not wait for your accounts to be completed and in most cases you will be expected to make installments based on assessments of your expected income and once your accounts are finalised you will then be informed of any over or under payment.

## Capital Gains Tax

If you have successfully bought and sold investments, antiques and property etc., you may find that you would be liable for capital gains tax.

Everyone is allowed to make a profit on opportunities that they fund with their own capital. There is, however, a limit, which you should check with the Inland Revenue, and any profit/gain that exceeds that figure would be liable for capital gains tax at the individual's marginal rate.

## Inheritance Tax

The subject of death is one which is rarely discussed openly and inheritance tax is thought to be an issue that is largely limited to the wealthy. This however, is a misconception, as inheritance tax will affect more people now than ever before.

In order to establish whether you are going to have an inheritance tax bill, you must assess the total value of the estate left by the deceased. This would include all assets and any gifts made within the preceding seven years. If the total figure exceeds £275.000 there will be a liability on the surplus of 40%. If the estate totals less than £275,000 there will be no liability. You should check these limits with the Inland Revenue as they are subject to change.

It now becomes clear that if you have been able to build a reasonable amount of savings, paid off your mortgage and may have received a pension lump sum and an inheritance yourself, you could be bordering on the £275,000 limit and your estate would be liable for inheritance tax. You should not restrict your own lifestyle in order to reduce your beneficiaries' tax bill but if you can afford it there are various options and exemptions that could substantially reduce the future liability.

## Exemptions

1. There is no inheritance tax between husband and wife.

2. To a U.K charity.

3. Gifts that total £3,000 a year.

4. £250 gifts made to anyone and however many people you like. This cannot be given to the same people as the £3,000.

5. Wedding presents, £5,000 from a parent, £2,500 from a grandparent, £1,000 from friend or family.

6. Part of a divorce settlement.

7. To support female parent-in-law if she is divorced, widowed or separated.

8. Selected agricultural land or business assets and unquoted shares.

## Gifts made seven years before death

Any gifts that the deceased made in the last 7 years of his or her life will be liable to inheritance tax on a sliding scale and the value of the gift will also form part of the estate.

In order to reduce the liability you could write any life insurance policies you have under trust and should you die, the benefits of your policies would not form part of your estate, but be payable to your spouse or children, therefore avoiding possible inheritance tax.

See also the importance of wills and trusts in chapter eleven.

# 11
# Wills and Trusts

Having an up-to-date Will is the only way to make sure that your possessions go where you want them to when you die. Without a Will, your house, savings, investments, car and other belongings will be left to the law to share out.

In your Will you can clearly and precisely state how you wish all your property to pass on your death.

When you make a Will you are showing, in a very practical way, that you care for those closest to you. By putting your affairs in order and making your wishes clearly known, you can save time, worry and unnecessary legal expenses for your family and friends.

**Example**

A married couple living together may each wish to make Wills naming the other as the executor and the beneficiary. The executor is a person nominated to carry out the instructions in the Will and the beneficiary is the person or persons to whom the estate is to go to.

In addition provision can be made that in the event of the death of both husband and wife then a third party will inherit the estate (for example the parents of both husband and wife).

In most cases this is a fairly straightforward procedure and the cost of preparing a Will of this nature will average around £40.00 plus VAT for both husband and wife.

## If a Will is not made

If you do not make a Will your estate will devolve according to intestacy rules laid down by parliament. Only people who are related to you by blood or a legal husband or wife can inherit from you. This could mean that the person who becomes entitled to the bulk of your estate may not be the person you wish to benefit, or your next of kin is prejudiced by the way the law of intestacy distributes your estate.

**Changing your Will**

Your Will is valid from the moment it is prepared, signed and witnessed in accordance with the law. You can at any time amend the terms of your original Will. If the changes are minor then you can execute a codicil which is a document read along side the original Will. However, in most cases it will be necessary for you to prepare a new Will which will then become operative in place of the old will.

**Benefits of making a Will**

In your Will you can nominate a person or persons to carry out your wishes and arrange for the distribution of your estate. If you do not nominate such a person an administrator must be nominated by law. This can slow down the administration and the delay may prejudice the needs of your immediate family.

If you have children you can ensure that they have a say in who looks after them by appointing testamentary guardians. This means that someone will be legally responsible for the children and avoids uncertainty in family argument.

If you are in the relevant "Tax Bracket" it may be possible to reduce inheritance tax liability on death with some simple tax planning in your Will.

A Will will enable you to leave a gift to a good cause or a close friend. The intestacy rules will not benefit a brother or sister of other close relative if your parents still live on after your death.

## Trusts

The principal uses of trusts today are:

1. To enable property to be held for persons who cannot themselves hold it, e.g. an infant or a person whose name may not be on the title deeds.
2. To tie up property so that it can benefit persons in succession. This means that a gift of property can be made to trustees to hold upon trust for life (their lifetime) and upon their death to go to that person's child.
3. To make a gift in the future in the light of circumstances which have not yet arisen.
4. To make provision, particularly by Will, for causes or non-human objects. By means of a trust one may donate money for the furtherance of education, or to provide a daily saucer of milk for "my tomcat Tiddles so long as he shall live".
5. To enable two or more persons to own land.
6. To minimise the incidence of income tax, capital gains tax and capital transfer tax.

One of the great advantages of a trust is the flexibility of purpose for which it can be used.

The cost involved in preparing a trust document will depend on the time spent preparing the deed and the complexity of the document.

# 12
# Borrowing money

Every year, according to statistics, we are borrowing more and more money. Indeed, if we look at the papers we can see that we are a 'nation in debt'. However, if you can possibly avoid credit, it is much better to do so. When you buy goods on credit or you borrow money you are, in most cases, taking out a high interest loan. It is the aim of banks to sell money for the highest rate possible in order to make profits. The best bet, at the end of the day, is the consumer. Better than the stock market or any other investment.

Obviously, in some cases you will need to borrow money. The main point is that, if you do have to borrow get the best deal possible. Read the small print. It is really surprising how few people shop around for a good deal and end up paying over the odds.

## Caution before you borrow

One question that you need to ask yourself before you borrow is: do I really need to borrow? Many people are tempted to borrow money even when they have money saved. This is mainly because it is a nice feeling having money in the bank. However, this is an illusion. The interest you pay on your borrowings will always be more than the savings. To borrow when you have enough in the bank to pay for an item is false economy.

If you do not have savings you should think very carefully about whether you really need to spend the money now or whether you can wait. If borrowing is absolutely necessary it is important to know what repayments you can afford. The quicker you can clear a loan the less you will pay. Once you have run up credit, make repaying it a priority.

**Comparisons of costs**

It is a fact that any lender will be happy to give you credit, providing that you are seen as creditworthy. If you are in the process of getting a loan make sure that you have shopped around, including using the Internet. To find the cheapest credit you will need to compare different lenders interest rates in the form of their APR (Annual Percentage Rate). The APR is designed to show the true cost of borrowing, and all lenders must calculate it the same way. Arrangement fees and any other charges must be included in the calculation as well as interests. How and when payments are made is also taken into account. This allows you to make direct comparisons between different forms of borrowing, so check that you are being quoted the APR and not the monthly rate of interest which sounds a lot less but is usually more.

Generally, the lower the APR. the lower the cost of credit, but make sure that the deals that you compare are for the same repayment period. The APR, as the name implies, is the cost of credit over one year at a time. If you spread the repayment of a loan over two years the cost will be more than one year even if the APR is lower.

The APR may not be the only factor to take into account when comparing loans. Some lenders will reduce the APR if you take out protection insurance, usually making the overall package more expensive. You should also consider whether rates are fixed or variable. Fixed rates protect you from rate rises and enable you to budget but your payments won't fall either. If rates are reduced your payments are fixed and will not reduce. This is very much a calculation that you have to make. In today's low interest rate climate it may be that any further reduction may be so negligible as not to affect your judgment.

**Payment protection insurance**

Payment protection insurance is usually offered with credit nowadays. This again is down to your own judgment. Without a doubt this insurance is useful if you are unemployed or have an accident and cannot pay the loans.

**Borrowing to pay off other loans**

We are bombarded with moneylenders, or their agents (companies set up to sell money on behalf of others) who tell us how prudent it is to put all your eggs in one basket. This normally involves re-mortgaging. You should try to restrict yourself to conventional lenders. In many cases, it will appear cheaper in the short-term to borrow money over a long period. You will save on the monthly outgoings but pay a lot more over the period of the loan. If you need to go down this route you will probably find that re-mortgaging with a bank or building society will be a lot cheaper than a secured loan.

**Overdrafts**

If you want to borrow for a short period an authorised overdraft will be a good option, providing that your bank offers competitive terms. Some banks charge arrangement fees for borrowing others will apply relatively high rates. Many will have a combination of both. If you overdraw without permission, which the banks favour, the interest rates charged will double. The advantages of overdrafts are that they are flexible but the amounts that you can borrow are limited.

**Credit cards**

Credit cards are one of the easiest and most popular ways of borrowing money. They are convenient and flexible and there is no need to approach the lender other than in the first instance when applying for a card. Maximum limits vary depending on your own circumstances, but can be between £1000 and £15000 usually. The balance that you run up on your card can be paid as quickly or slowly as you wish subject to a monthly limit, usually 3% or £5 whichever is the lower.

If you clear your monthly balance in full there will be no interest charge. This means that you can gain up to 59 days interest free credit between the time that the transaction took place and the time that it takes you to pay the bill. If you do not pay the balance in full then interest is charged.

Interest rates on credit cards vary greatly. They can range between 5-20% and more, depending on the deal on offer. Many card companies try to attract customers by offering reduced rates on balance transfers. Some give these low introductory rates on new purchases as well. The introductory rate usually lasts six months. This can be useful if you want to spread the payments over a few months but contain the interest payment.

Buying goods and services by credit card can make sense in other ways. If you use your card to buy something worth between £100 and £30,000 you will normally qualify for extra protection under section 75 of the Consumer Credit Act, which makes the card issuer jointly liable with the supplier if there is a problem with the goods. Other perks can also be offered by the card supplier such as free travel insurance.

### Personal loans

Personal loans are offered by many organisations nowadays, with the large supermarkets and insurance companies getting in on the act. These lenders can usually offer competitive rates. So can lenders over the internet. If you want to make a major purchase the vendor will usually offer to arrange a loan but it may be more competitive to seek a personal loan elsewhere.

Personal loans are a useful way of borrowing over the medium term if you cannot get an overdraft to cover the period. Between £5000 and £25000 can normally be obtained over periods of 1-25 years. The more you borrow the lower the APR. You should always carefully scrutinise the rates on offer and don't be misled. If you need a borrowing facility that you can re-use, rather than a one-off sum, some lenders offer flexible loans where you agree a monthly payment and are allowed to borrow a maximum multiple of that amount at any time.

**Secured or unsecured loans**

Most personal loans are unsecured. This means that if you do not pay the lender can take you to court but does not have the right to seize any property or possessions. With a secured loan assets such as property (usually property) are used, as security and the lender will take a second charge on your property for the value of the loan. This is known as a second charge loan. Nowadays, there is little advantage in taking out a secured loan as you may be able to find a better rate for unsecured loans, unless you have a poor credit rating.

**Interest free or low start credit**

This type of credit often seems too good to be true. Many people take it up, particularly on cars or furniture. However, nothing is free and you should look carefully at the terms and conditions. You could find that you are signing up to an interest-bearing loan, with interest waived only if you pay up in full during an initial period. If you miss the deadline to pay of the balance then hefty interest charges will be incurred.

The main principle is that you should always check very carefully what it is that you are getting into.

## Hire purchase

Hire purchase is still one of the most common forms of car finance. There are several important differences between hire purchase and personal loans: first, unlike a loan which can cover the whole cost, a cash deposit is normally required with hire purchase. This can also be the part exchange value of your car. Secondly, you are effectively hiring the goods rather than acquiring ownership. This means that until the final payment is made the goods do not belong to you. If you fail to make payments the gods will be repossessed.

## Credit Unions

Credit unions are becoming an increasingly important low cost way of borrowing money, particularly for people who find conventional borrowing difficult to access. Essentially, credit unions are financial co-operatives set up and run by people with some sort of common bond. Members may work together or belong to the same profession or live on the same estate. The main principle is co-operation.

Members who save regularly are able to get cheap loans. Apart from the low cost you don't need an established credit record to borrow, your savings record and ability to pay will be the main factors when applying for a loan. To find out if there is a credit union you can join, or how to set one up, contact the Association of British Credit Unions.

## If you are turned down for credit

Lenders cannot refuse credit on factors such as race, gender or other but they can turn down your application if they think that you may not be able to repay your debt. Lenders usually make a decision as to your credit worthiness by a means of 'credit scoring' and/or by contacting a credit reference agency.

**Credit scoring.**

Lenders score you on the basis of answers given on your application form. They take into account factors such as whether you own your home or rent, salary, age and occupation. Only those applicants who score above a certain level are deemed credit worthy.

With credit reference agencies, there are a number of specialist organisations which collect factual information about individuals which they pass onto lenders. Their data comes from the electoral roll, other lenders and the courts. This enables potential lenders to find out whether you have defaulted on any other credit agreements, have any County Court Judgments or are bankrupt. Negative information will stay on record for six years. If you are refused credit on the basis of information gained from an agency the lender will give you the name and address of the agency used. You can then contact the agency, with details of yourself and addresses lived in over the last six years and they will supply information. If you find that the information is incorrect then you can ask for it to be corrected and the agency must send the file to any organisation that has asked for it over the last six months.

# 13
# Education

With the huge variety of standards in education in different state schools, sometimes parents think that the only option is to educate their children privately at a fee-paying school. Fee-paying schools are used more and more by different socio-economic groups who have built up the fees through a private savings scheme. The number of fee paying schools has grown to a point where nearly 600,000 children are educated there, out of a total of 8.2 million children in receipt of education.

Obviously, fee-paying schools are still going to be the preserve of those who can afford them but this chapter gives an insight into planning for the fees. Fees can vary: at one end of the scale, the cheaper end, it can cost £10,000 per year per child. At the upper end, the Eton's of this world, the fees are much higher. If you are intent on sending your child(ren) to a fee paying school then the only way to do so is to save from the child early age.

If you are fortunate enough to earn enough to save for the Childs education then you will be looking to invest a regular amount or a lump sum into an investment product that will, hopefully, grow at a rate higher than inflation. This could be:

- A savings account or National Savings Certificate (low risk)
- An investment or unit trust (medium to high risk)
- A bond fund (medium to low risk)
- A fixed term annuity (low risk)
- Zero preference shares

Zero preference shares are shares from an investment trust that has split itself into two types of shares. One produces capital growth but zero income. And the other just takes the income. The term 'preference shares means that should the trust go bankrupt these shares get paid before other shares on the creditors list. You would need sound financial advice before purchasing these shares.

Your savings should be invested in as tax efficient a manner as possible, probably ISA or a children's bond. You should also be aware that gifts to a child from someone other than its parents could be tax efficient, as children have their own income tax thresholds so can earn up to that threshold without incurring tax liability (currently £4750 per annum)

It is recommended that parents start to invest for their children's school fees as soon as a child arrives as obviously the longer that you save the more money you will have. At pre-school and prep-school, fees are smaller than secondary fees and it may be possible for you to pay for them out of income and continue to contribute to a savings scheme.

Many schools offer composition fee schemes, where you start paying to the school before the child gets there. This forward paying entitles you to significant discounts from the school. However, these are only useful if your child attends that particular school. You will not receive interest on the money and will lose out if at the last moment you decide not to send your child to that school.

When advance planning for school fees there are a number of points to consider:

- It can be very disruptive to a Childs education to remove them from a school where they have settled in, so make sure you can afford the fees on an ongoing basis.

- School fees tend to increase faster than the rate of inflation, so make your calculation allowing for an increase of 5% per year.
- You will need to plan for all your children. Make an assumption if you don't know how many you will have.
- Be aware of your own likely income growth.

## Bursaries, scholarships and other help

Most independent schools have schemes where help is available to pay fees. They are often small amounts, amounting to several hundred pounds or less. This might make a difference however, if you are having difficulty paying fees. Scholarships are usually for more generous amounts and are awarded to children with talents deemed to be worth developing and supporting. In addition, educational trusts do exist and you might find it useful to make enquiries about these to a local education authority.

If you want more information about investing for school fees and the names of suitable advisors The Independent Schools information service (ISCs) can give you names of suitable firms. They can be found at www.iscis.uk.net and the ISC London and South East Office on 020 7798 1561.

## University education

The whole area of university funding has changed in the last 20 years or so and it is now costly to send a child to university. Most parents of children who now go to university received a grant and, other than getting part time work, received their education for free (if they went to university). Now, a contribution to education and maintenance is necessary. The burden of fees and maintenance is now largely met through student loans which only have to be repaid on leaving university. This means that the child will be liable to repay its own loan on leaving university. However, many parents wish to help and again a plan is necessary.

**Current costs of university**

At current costs it is estimated that £23,000 will be needed over a three-year period, this is without university vacations. This relates to £7600 per year approximately. Some degrees can last considerably longer. The £7600 is comprised of the following:

Rent £2000
Food and essentials £1200
Utilities and insurance £450
Travel £500
Books etc £450
Clothing and cleaning £450
Tuition fees £1,100
Leisure £1400

It must be borne in mind that accommodation off-campus can be more expensive especially in larger cities. In out of control rent environments such as London this needs some careful thought.

**Future costs**

The government is proposing to introduce a graduate tax from 2006, where universities will be allowed to 'top up' the current tuition fee of £1100 by up to a further £1900 giving a ceiling of £3000 for tuition fees per student per year. It is expected that the more prestigious universities will charge the full amount. The effects of this top up are that it will, more than likely, add another £6000 of debt to a three-year course.

**Student Loan Company**

The government has operated its student loan scheme through the Student Loan Company since 1990. For loans taken out by students prior to the academic year 1998, the loans were applied for directly through the SLC and collected by the SLC following graduation, once the graduate was earning over £1752 gross per moth. Now the situation is more complex. Students must apply for support (no longer referred to as a loan) assessments from their local Education Authority (in England and Wales) the Student Award Agency for Scotland (does not apply to domiciled students studying in Scotland there is a different system in place whereby a fixed amount is paid back at the end of the degree)) or the Education and Library Boards in Northern Ireland, depending on residence not proposed university. These bodies make an assessment of the support requirements including parental income. Collection of the support is now done by employers through the Inland Revenue. Payment is at 9% per year once income is over 10% gross. The Student Loans Company still makes the payments and administers loans. Loans are allocated on a year-by-year basis not for the duration of the whole course.

As we have seen above, the outcome of a university education is that students are saddled with debt. Any help that can be given parentally is obviously a bonus. The ways of saving for university fees are the same as saving for other school fees. However, you need to be in a position where you can do this. If you are on the point of sending a child to university then you should make full enquiries to the university of choice about any extra help available if you are on a low income.

# 14
# Health care

Healthcare is one of the most contentious issues in modern day society. It is always in the news and it is used as an ongoing political football. The government tries to provide healthcare 'free at the point of delivery' and to a large extent achieves this aim. However, it is true to say that we are living longer than we used to and we are suffering more diseases and incapacities as a result. This means that the NHS has to treat more people than ever before, and there are greater pressures financially and organisationally.

## Private medical care and insurance

In certain cases, it is an advantage to have private medical insurance as you will be able to exercise more choice over where and when you are treated instead of waiting in line with other people to treat what may be a painful condition. The drawback is that private medical care does not come cheap.

It is said that for people under forty, on the whole, private medical care insurance provides poor value for money. It is over the age of forty that insurance starts to provide real benefits. It is estimated that on average people in their twenties and thirties will have in patient treatment once every ten years. The cost of that treatment averages £2000. The costs of premiums over ten years will be in the region of £5000 so the outcome is that you invest more than you get out. Of course, it may be that a serious condition occurs and that you are achieving value for money. However, it is the over-forties who tend to benefit more. Over forty though, premiums start to rise.

If you decide that you want to get private medical insurance there are certain key decisions that you might want to make. If relevant, you should see whether your employer offers such insurance. This is the cheapest option. If, however, this is not an option you will need to shop around for the best deal. Most insurance companies will offer PMI and it is usually through the larger providers of treatment such as BUPA. When selecting which level of cover is appropriate for you, you will be offered a wide range of options. The three standard areas of cover are:

- In-patient treatment (where you stay in hospital overnight or longer)
- Day-patient treatment (where you require supervised recovery time but do not stay overnight
- Out-patient treatment (where you get treatment at a consulting room or surgery)

Generally, most good policies will cover all eventualities but you may have to pay more for out-patient treatment. Other choices you will have to make are:

- Whether you wish unlimited care or a certain amount of cover each year
- Whether you wish to go to any private hospital of your choice or from a selection offered by the insurance company
- Whether cover is only offered is the NHS cannot provide cover within a given period of time (typically 6-12 weeks)
- The size of excess you are willing to pay
- The opportunity to pay for a certain part of the treatment yourself such as consultation)

When applying for PMI you will be required to make a statement about your current health and any previous conditions you may have had. Failure to disclose such conditions can void your policy.

There is a standard list of conditions that insurers tend not to cover. The Association of British Insurers list the following:

- Pre-existing conditions
- GP services
- Long term (chronic illness)
- Accident and emergency admissions
- Drug abuse
- HIV/AIDS
- Infertility
- Normal pregnancy
- Cosmetic surgery
- Gender realignment
- Preventive treatment
- Kidney dialysis
- Mobility aids
- Experimental treatment
- Experimental drugs
- Organ transplant
- War risks
- Injuries arising from dangerous hobbies

**Regulatory structure**

Almost all PMI providers in the UK are members of the Association of British Insurers (ABI) and registered with the General Insurance Standards Council (GISC). You should check that your provider is registered before signing up to any scheme. If you have any complaint you should take it up with your insurance provider first. If it does not satisfy you, you can then go to the GISC (tell 0845 601 2857) or www.gisc.co.uk. The FSA has taken over general insurance regulation from January 2005.

## Long term care

The issue of long-term care is a relatively new one for the finance industry and is little understood by the general public. The structures of the industry and state provision are complex and there are many firms who fail to attain high standards.

Many of us will need long term care in old age. LTC comes in two forms: home care where individuals are looked after in their own homes; and care homes where people go into residential care.

Home care services range from meals on wheels, home alterations to community nursing and day care and respite centres. Local authorities provide the majority of these, but the NHS is responsible for certain areas. The NHS aid is free but usually only available when it is proved that it can improve the patient's medical condition. The general overall rule is that the majority of money is spent on those people most in need.

## LTC insurance

These are 'pre-funded' policies where you purchase the cover through payment of regular premiums or with a one-off lump sum payment. You can start the policy at any age, although some insurers only offer policies to people over 40 or 50.

You will decide at the outset as to whether the policy will cover all your LTC expenses or just up to a specified amount and whether it will be a fixed level of insurance or will increase with inflation. Most policies are straightforward insurance only, but you can apply for an investment policy which will pay a capital sum at the end of the term or when you die should you have not used it in all claims. These policies tend to be more expensive.

These are certain risks with LTC insurance:

- The main risk is that you may never need it and if you die before claiming or you stay healthy then the premiums will have been wasted.
- Other risks are that you are purchasing cover for some years in the future (hopefully). It is quite possible that the level of cover may be insufficient for LTC needs. Your insurance company should review the cover every five years.
- The provision of LTC insurance can affect any means tested benefits the state may provide in the future
- Certain illness and disabilities might not be covered. For example mental illness may not be covered.
- Some policies only pay out for a limited time period but most should pay as long as required. This should be checked out when taking out the policy.

The cost of LTCI will depend on age, sex and state of health when taking out the policy.

**Immediate needs policies**

The downside, as mentioned, of LTCI is that you may never have to claim. Insurance companies will profit out of you. However, this is the risk with most types of insurance. An alternative to funding an ongoing policy is to take out an immediate needs policy.

Immediate needs policies are usually a variant of impaired life annuities. Life annuities are financial policies where in return for your paying a lump sum now, an insurance company guarantees to pay you a regular income each month for the rest of your life. With impaired life annuities insurers tend to be more generous as your life span is considered to be less than it should be.

There are two usual ways to pay for immediate needs policies: with a cash lump sum, or, popularly these days, with equity release. The benefits should be the same as they are determined by the annuity.

These policies are less risky than pre-funded policies as you only purchase one when you know you need it (they are not available until you have a need). However, they are more expensive as the insurance company is almost certain to have to pay you something, although it doesn't know how long. In most cases, when you have purchased an annuity you do not get money back other than the payments. As a result your estate could lose out after your death. Some policies will offer death benefits which are paid out regardless of when the policyholder dies.

## Regulators, advisers and providers

From November 2004 the FSA will regulate LTCI provision. This means that all new financial advisors will need to undergo training on LTC issues.

# 15
# Funeral costs and pre-paid plans

There are three things that must be done when someone dies:

- The death has to be certified by a doctor or coroner
- The death has to be registered with the Registrar of Births, Deaths and Marriages
- The body must be buried or cremated

It is not obligatory to have a funeral ceremony at all, nor is it essential to use a funeral director. However, the vast majority of people do have a ceremony and use a funeral director which is costly.

With the average cremation costing over £1500 and a burial over £2000 some planning for this cost can be worthwhile. Having established what type of funeral you want, it may be necessary to consider how it is to be paid for. One common method is for a pre-paid funeral plan, which can be obtained through many funeral directors. The advantage of a pre-paid plan is that there is the time to look around and get the best deal. The problem with these plans is that they have not always paid out as expected. Typically there are two parts to a funerals cost: the funeral directors costs, and then extra charges from doctor's fees to payment of all the charges associated with burial or cremation (grave diggers, headstones, burial plot, flowers, cremation fee and so on). A pre-paid plan will almost certainly cover the cost of the funeral director but should be checked carefully as to what other costs are covered.

To ensure that you get what you expect, check the following:

- Critically, check that your payment goes into a trust fund that is accounted for separately from the funeral planning company.
- Check that your plan will cover everything that you need to be covered.
- Does the plan cover the cost of a specified funeral director charges, regardless of price increases? Will it cover any funeral director?
- If you are paying by installments what happens if you die before all installments are paid?
- Can you change the plan to another funeral director or get a refund if you move to another part of the country?
- Does the plan cover removal of a body 'out of hours' (at night) or on holidays?
- Does the plan include removal of the body from anywhere in the UK?
- Is the funeral planning company part of a recognised trade organisation with an enforceable code of conduct such as the National Association of Pre-paid Funerals?

The FSA now covers the pre-paid funeral plan sector.

# 16
# The Costs of getting married

One event which usually figures large in any family, is that of one of the offspring getting married. It also figures large in the lives of those who embark on a second or subsequent marriage. In this chapter we look in detail at the costs involved.

The average cost of getting married in 2004 was £16,000. That seems a high figure and we will look at just how the costs can escalate. It is true to say that, because of the high cost, many couples look for an alternative to the traditional lavish wedding, such as a registry office, which may not be so social and romantic but will leave you in pocket.

What follows is an examination of three types of wedding and the costs associated with each.

## Economy wedding

This involves the use of a registry office and a reception afterwards. The total cost is around £450. Registry office fees cost around £100. These tend to change and you should enquire at the local office in your area. The £100 comprises £30 each for a notice of marriage and £37.50 for a certificate of marriage.

You should expect to spend around £150 on clothes for the occasion unless you wear existing clothes. £100 is budgeted for rings, something simple. A further £100 is spent on food and wine for a reception at home.

This kind of wedding will not be suitable for all but it shows that getting married need not break the bank. It really depends on the attitude of the couple in question and, perhaps, other factors such as family pressures.

## Traditional wedding

This is where the costs can mount up. It is where a good deal of pre-planning needs to happen and perhaps some prudent budgeting way before the event.

A traditional wedding will cost you somewhere in the region of £12,500. The average cost is around £16,000, according to research by the magazine 'You and Your Wedding'. Major expenses include:

Bride: dress and other clothing: £1500
Bridegroom: clothes £450
Bridesmaid outfits: £400
Flowers for bridal party and venue: £450
Wedding cars: £500
Hire of country hotel for reception: £1400
Catering for 80 guests: £2500
Drinks: £1300
Photography and video: £1400
Entertainment and music £550
Church ceremony legal fees: £219.50
Publication of bans: £18
Marriage service: £198
Marriage certificate: £3.50
Bell ringers and organist: £100
Stationary and invitations: £250
Tiered wedding cake: £250
Gifts for bridesmaids: £100

Total: £11754.

There will be other costs along the way. If you are set on a traditional wedding you should budget £12000 minimum. As we have seen throughout this book there are many ways of saving for the future and, if you are prudent, you will want to begin investing money early to ensure that you can give your son or daughter a marriage that they never forget.

**Luxury wedding**

If you are lucky enough to be in a position where no expense is spared then you might want to choose from the growing number of wedding coordinators to plan the day for you. This will spare you the headache and ensure a fabulous wedding. The average coordinator will charge around 15% of the budget. The costs of such a wedding can be anything up to £150,000. I will not go into a detailed breakdown of costs of such a wedding for two reasons: you can obtain a breakdown tailored to your requirements from a wedding coordinator. In addition, if a reader of this book were in the position to spend such an amount then they would not be reading this book. A wedding at this figure could pay for a flat or house for the lucky couple.

There are many ways to keep costs of a wedding down without coming across as a cheapskate. You should haggle for good deals with suppliers, ask friends who have recently got married about any bargains they have found. Winter, midweek and Sunday weddings cost less than summer Saturday weddings. Instead of hiring a venue tailor made hire an empty venue and organize your own reception. Afternoon weddings usually mean big savings. The limited hours will reduce your food and drinks budget. Keep your wedding small as many weddings are charged on a per guest basis. Only invite 'A' list friends and relatives. There are many little things that you can do to save thousands of pounds, which can be spent on much needed items later on.

## Useful addresses and websites

## The regulation of financial advice

The Financial Services Authority
25 The North Colonnade
Canary Wharf
London E14 5HS
Public enquiries helpline 0845 606 1234
www.fsa.gov.uk
Consumer helpline email:consumerhelp@fsa.gov.uk

**Ombudsman**
The Financial Ombudsman Service
South Quay Plaza
183 Marsh Wall
London E14 9SR
Tel: 0845 080 1800
www.financial-ombudsman.org.uk

The above deals with complaints about individual pensions and free standing AVC's, life insurance, general insurance and investment products.

**Other ombudsmen, complaints and advice schemes**
The Pensions Ombudsman
11 Belgrave Road
London SW1V 1RB
020 7834 9144
www.pensions-ombudsman.org.uk
The above deals with complaints about occupational pension schemes.

The Office for the Pensions Advisory Service Opas
11 Belgrave Road
London SW1V 1RB
020 7233 8080

www.opas.org.uk
For advice about occupational and personal pension schemes.

The Occupational Pensions Regulatory Authority (Opra)
Invicta House
Trafalgar Place
Brighton BN1 4DW
001273 627600

www.opra.gov.uk
www.stakeholder.opra.gov.uk
For general complaints about the running of company pension schemes.

The Office for the Supervision of Solicitors
Victoria Court
8 Dormer Place
Leamington Spa
Warwick CV32 5AE
01926 822007

The Ombudsman for Estate Agents
Beckett House
4 Bridge Street
Salisbury Wilts SP1 2LX
01722 333306

The Mortgage Code Arbitration Scheme
11 Bloomsbury Square
London WC1A 2LT
020 7421 7444

The General Insurance Standards Council
110 Cannon Street
London EC4N 6EU
0845 601 2857
www.gisc.co.uk

**Pensions and retirement**

The Pension Schemes Registry
PO Box 1NN
Newcastle under Tyne
NE9 1N
0191 225 6316

To track down old company pension schemes

The Pre-retirement Association
9 Chesham Road
Guildford
Surrey GU1 3LS
01483 301170
www.pra.uk.com

The Pensions Compensation Board
11 Belgrave Road
London SW1V 1RB
020 7828 9794

## Financial Advisers

IFA Promotion
17-19 Emery Road
Brislington
Bristol BS4 5PF
0800 085 3250

www.ifap.org.uk

The Money Management Directory of fee based Advisers
C/O Matrix Data Services
Freepost 22
London W1E 1BR
0870 013 1925

www.uk/fadirectory.co.uk

The Association of Private Client Investment managers and Stockbrokers (APCIMS)
112 Middlesex Street
London E1 7HY
020 7247 70870

www.apcims.co.uk

The Society of Financial Advisers (Sofa)
20 Aldermanbury
London EC2V 7HY
020 7417 4442

www.sofa.org

The Association of Solicitor Investment managers (ASIM)
Chiddingstone Causeway
Tonbridge
Kent TN11 8JX
01892 870065

www.asim.org.uk

Solicitors for Independent Advice4
10 East Street
Epsom
Surrey KT17 1HH
01372 721172

www.solicitor-ifa.co.uk

The Association of Pension Lawyers
C/O Pinsent Curtis Biddle
1 Gresham Street
London EC2V 7BU
020 7418 700

www.apl.org.uk

The Ethical Investment Research Service
80-84 Bondway
London SW8 1SF
0845 606 0324

www.eiris.org

## Accountants

The Institute of Chartered Accountants in England and Wales
Moorgate Place
London EC2P 2BJ
020 7920 8100

www.icaew.co.uk

The Institute of Chartered Accountants in Scotland
21 Haymarket Yards
Edinburgh EH12 5BH
0131 347 0100

www.icas.org.uk

The Association of Chartered Certified Accountants
29 Lincoln's In Fields
London WC2A 3EE
020 7396 7000

www.accaglobal.com

The Chartered Institute of Taxation and The Association of Tax Technicians
12 Upper Belgrave Street
London SW1X 8B
020 7235 9381

www.tax.org.uk

## Specialist Magazines

Money Management
3rd Floor
Maple House
149 Tottenham Court Road
London W1P 9LL
020 7896 2525

Planned Savings
6-77 Paul Street
London EC2A 4LG
020 753 1000
Money management and Planned Savings are aimed at professional advisers.

Moneyfacts
Moneyfacts House
6-70 Thorpe Road
Norwich NR1 1BJ
01603 476476

www.moneyfacts.co.uk

This magazine publishes a monthly round up of all savings account rates. For more up-to-date listings see the web site.

## Trade Bodies

The Association of Investment Trust Companies
Durrant House
8-13 Chiswell Street
London EC21Y 4YY
0800 085 8520

www.itsonline.co.uk www.aitc.co.uk

Provides information on aspects of investing in investment trust companies.

The Investment Management Association
65 Kingsway
London WC2B 6TD
020 8207 1361

www.investmentuk.org
Provides information on investing in unit trusts and Oeics

Proshare
Centurion House
24 Monument Street
London EC2R 8AQ
020 7394 5200

www.proshare.org.uk

Advises on setting up investment clubs and runs education programmes for schools on share ownership

The Association of British Insurers
61 Gresham Street
London EC2V 7HQ
020 7600 333

www.abi.org.uk
Publishes information sheets on all aspects of insurance.

The British Insurance Brokers Association

14 Bevis Marks
London EC3A 7NT
020 7623 9043

www.biba.org.uk

The Building Societies Association
3 Savile Row
London W1S 3PB
020 7437 0655

www.bsa.org.uk

The Council of Mortgage Lenders
3 Savile Row
London W1S 3BP
020 7437 0655

The National Association of Estate Agents
Arbon House
21 Jury Street
Warwick CV34 4EH
01926 496800

www.naea.co.uk

The Royal Institution of Chartered Surveyors
12 Great George Street
Parliament Square
London SW1P 3AD
020 7222 7000
www.rics.org.uk
The Association of Residential Letting Agents

Maple House
53-5 Woodside Road
Amersham
Bucks HP6 6AA
01923 89655

www.aria.co.uk

**Borrowing**
The National Debtline
0808 808 4000

The Association of British Credit Unions
Holyoake House
Hanover Street
Manchester M60 OAS
0161 832 8694

www.abcul.org

**Credit Information Agencies**
Experian
Consumer help services
PO Box 8000
Nottingham NG1 5GX
0870 241 6212

www.experian.com

Equifax Europe (UK)
Credit file advice centre
PO Box 3001
Glasgow G81 0583

0870 010 0583
www.equifax.co.uk

## Investment information websites

www.investment-gateway.com
www.new-online-investor.co.uk
www.find.co.uk

**www.straightforwardco.co.uk**

All titles, listed below, in the Straightforward Guides Series can be purchased online, using credit card or other forms of payment by going to www.straightfowardco.co.uk A discount of 25% per title is offered with online purchases.

**Law**

*A Straightforward Guide to:*

Consumer Rights
Bankruptcy Insolvency and the Law
Employment Law
Private Tenants Rights
Family law
Small Claims in the County Court
Contract law
Intellectual Property and the law
Divorce and the law
Leaseholders Rights
The Process of Conveyancing
Knowing Your Rights and Using the Courts
Producing Your own Will
Housing Rights
The Bailiff the law and You
Probate and The Law
Company law
What to Expect When You Go to Court
Guide to Competition Law
Give me Your Money-Guide to Effective Debt Collection
Caring for a Disabled Child

**General titles**

Letting Property for Profit
Buying, Selling and Renting property
Buying a Home in England and France
Bookkeeping and Accounts for Small Business

Creative Writing
Freelance Writing
Writing Your own Life Story
Writing performance Poetry
Writing Romantic Fiction
Speech Writing

Teaching Your Child to Read and write
Teaching Your Child to Swim
Raising a Child-The Early Years

Creating a Successful Commercial Website
The Straightforward Business Plan
The Straightforward C.V.
Successful Public Speaking

Handling Bereavement
Play the Game-A Compendium of Rules
Individual and Personal Finance
Understanding Mental Illness
The Two Minute Message
Guide to Self Defence
Buying a Used Car
Tiling for Beginners

Go to:
www.straightforwardco.co.uk